Pyramids

New and future titles in the series include:

Alien Abductions

Angels

The Bermuda Triangle

The Curse of King Tut

Dragons

ESP

Extinction of the Dinosaurs

Haunted Houses

King Arthur

The Loch Ness Monster

Pyramids

UFOs

Vampires

Witches

The Mystery Library

Pyramids

Stuart A. Kallen

LUCENT BOOKS
SAN DIEGO, CALIFORNIA

THOMSON

GALE

Detroit • New York • San Diego • San Francisco
Boston • New Haven, Conn. • Waterville, Maine
London • Munich

Library of Congress Cataloging-in-Publication Data

Kallen, Stuart A., 1955–
    Pyramids / by Stuart A. Kallen.
      p. cm. — (The mystery library)
Includes bibliographical references and index.
Summary: Discusses the building, purpose, and mystical associations
of the Egyptian pyramids.
    ISBN 1-56006-773-X (hardback : alk. paper)
    1. Pyramids—Egypt—Juvenile literature. [1. Pyramids—
Egypt. 2. Egypt—Antiquities.] I. Title. II. Mystery library
(Lucent Books)
    DT63 K35 2002
    932—dc21

                       2001006608

Contents

Foreword

In Shakespeare's immortal play, *Hamlet*, the young Danish aristocrat Horatio has clearly been astonished and disconcerted by his encounter with a ghostlike apparition on the castle battlements. "There are more things in heaven and earth," his friend Hamlet assures him, "than are dreamt of in your philosophy."

Many people today would readily agree with Hamlet that the world and the vast universe surrounding it are teeming with wonders and oddities that remain largely outside the realm of present human knowledge or understanding. How did the universe begin? What caused the dinosaurs to become extinct? Was the lost continent of Atlantis a real place or merely legendary? Does a monstrous creature lurk beneath the surface of Scotland's Loch Ness? These are only a few of the intriguing questions that remain unanswered, despite the many great strides made by science in recent centuries.

Lucent Books' Mystery Library series is dedicated to exploring these and other perplexing, sometimes bizarre, and often disturbing or frightening wonders. Each volume in the series presents the best-known tales, incidents, and evidence surrounding the topic in question. Also included are the opinions and theories of scientists and other experts who have attempted to unravel and solve the ongoing mystery. And supplementing this information is a fulsome list of sources for further reading, providing the reader with the means to pursue the topic further.

The Mystery Library will satisfy every young reader's fascination for the unexplained. As one of history's greatest scientists, physicist Albert Einstein, put it:

The most beautiful thing we can experience is the mysterious. It is the source of all true art and science. He to whom this emotion is a stranger, who can no longer wonder and stand rapt in awe, is as good as dead: his eyes are closed.

Mysteries in Stone

The ancient Egyptians began building pyramids around forty-nine hundred years ago; between approximately 2900 B.C. and 1500 B.C. almost one hundred of the structures were built. Many have fallen into rubble and today are barely identifiable as pyramids. Others, such as those in Giza, near present-day Cairo, are relatively intact and are considered among the greatest wonders on earth.

Constructed around 2550 B.C. from millions of limestone blocks—each weighing nearly three tons—the Great Pyramid of King Khufu (or Cheops) at Giza rises 481 feet above the desert floor. Each side of its square base is 756 feet in length. And for more than forty-four centuries—until 1887, when the Eiffel Tower was constructed in Paris—the Great Pyramid was the tallest structure on earth.

While there is no denying the stunning physical reality of these massive stone monuments, they are surrounded by mysteries, some as old as the pyramids themselves. For example, the ancient Egyptians left no record of how the pyramids were constructed, what tools were used, how many laborers performed the work, or in some cases even exactly who ordered them built.

Since the early nineteenth century, however, thousands of scholars, known as Egyptologists, who study the pyramids and other aspects of ancient Egyptian civilization, have advanced various theories to explain the mystery of these massive monuments. Still, much remains unexplained. For instance, no one has ever answered how the heavy stones used in pyramid construction were moved. The exact age of the pyramids remains a mystery, as does the exact purpose the stone monuments were supposed to fulfill. And the fact that the monuments were built over a widely dispersed region, as opposed to one area, continues to puzzle researchers.

Pyramids have long been associated in the popular imagination with paranormal phenomena. As such, pyramids and "pyramid power" have generated thousands of claims and theories over the centuries. The magical powers of the pyramids have been associated with making plants grow, healing the sick, preserving food, and sharpening razor blades. Others have found connections between the pyramids and the lost city of Atlantis, biblical prophecy, and even space aliens.

Despite extensive research and study of the pyramids, mysteries remain regarding the building of these enormous stone monuments.

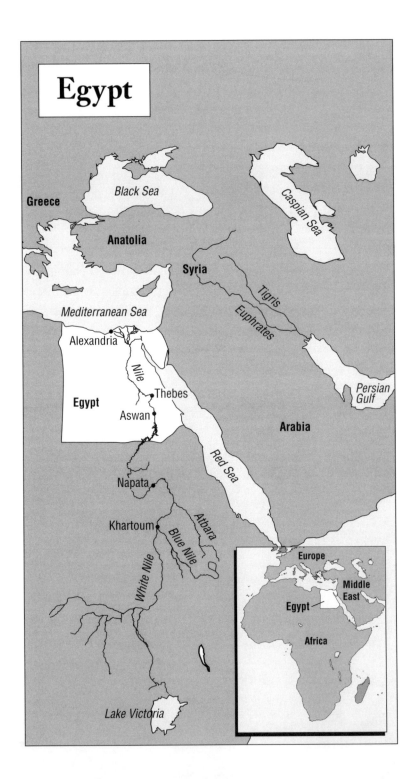

Egypt

Greece

Black Sea

Anatolia

Caspian Sea

Syria

Tigris

Euphrates

Mediterranean Sea

Alexandria

Nile

Egypt

Thebes

Aswan

Persian Gulf

Arabia

Red Sea

Napata

Khartoum

Atbara

Blue Nile

White Nile

Europe

Middle East

Egypt

Africa

Lake Victoria

The Land of the Pharaohs

That the puzzle of the pyramids has remained a topic of speculation for centuries should not be surprising. The ancient Egyptian civilization believed to be responsible for the pyramids was one of the most advanced societies known. And the Egyptians' complex and mysterious religious beliefs, of which pyramid building was believed to be a major part, have perplexed scholars for thousands of years. As Robert Bauval and Adrian Gilbert write in *The Orion Mystery: Unlocking the Secrets of the Pyramids:*

> [The] Egyptians were . . . an extremely reserved people, who kept the inner mysteries of their religion from all but a few chosen initiates. As it was these few who directed the building of the pyramids, is not surprising that we know so little about their motives. [1]

What is known is that the roots of civilization in Egypt date back more than nine thousand years, when people first began farming along the banks of the Nile River. The bond between the Nile and the Egyptians was very strong, as the river flooded the land every year between July and October, bringing fresh water and rich, fertile soil to the parched sandy desert where rain rarely fell.

Egyptians eventually built a civilization made up of two kingdoms—the Red Land of Upper Egypt in the south, and Black Land of Lower Egypt along the Nile Delta. About 3100 B.C., the ruler of Upper Egypt, King Menes ("the founder"), united the two kingdoms and became Egypt's first pharaoh. The capital was established at the city of Memphis, south of present-day Cairo.

Power was centralized in King Menes, who was a god-king—a ruler believed to be both a king and a deity. Menes, like all the pharaohs who followed, passed his ruling power along to his heirs when he died. These family members in turn passed their power down to their heirs. These ruling families were called dynasties; between 3100 B.C. and 332 B.C., Egypt was ruled by a succession of thirty such dynasties.

With the unification of the two lands under Menes, the glorious age of pharaohs began. Power was centralized and all of the growing country's economic, political, and religious institutions fell under royal authority. The central government employed soldiers, scholars, servants, bureaucrats, and artisans whose goods and services were used to benefit the upper classes and nobility. These workers also established a sophisticated tradition of art and learning that formed the basis of Egyptian civilization for many generations.

The pharaonic system enabled the ancient Egyptians to lead the world in innovation and invention. Even before Menes united the two lands, Egyptians had developed a type of plow and a system of writing. Egyptians were also the first to build in stone and to fashion arches with stone and brick.

Between 3100 and 2686 B.C.—periods known as the First Dynasty and Second Dynasty—Egyptians became accomplished shipbuilders and sailors. They charted the stars and planets in the heavens and thus were able to predict cyclical events, such as the annual flood of the Nile, and develop the concept of the year and the twelve monthly divisions of the calendar.

As ingenious as they were in the material realm, Egyptians believed that life on earth was only a part of an individual's total existence. After death, a person was believed to enter the afterlife for eternity. Central to Egyptian beliefs was the idea that how the dead were treated affected their existence in the afterlife.

The Pyramid Builders

With the beginning of the Third Dynasty in 2649 B.C., Egypt entered five centuries of high culture known as the Pyramid Age. Most of these pyramids were constructed on the west bank of the Nile, south of the delta, in a region approximately sixty miles long.

The earliest pharaohs built low, flat-topped mud-brick structures called mastabas, which featured slanting sides. The first pyramidlike building, known as the Step Pyramid, was

The Ancient Gods

Religious and poetic incantations written in the *Book of the Dead* were used to help deceased persons gain entrance into the afterlife. Egyptians believed that after death, the god Osiris and forty-two judges weighed the dead person's heart on a scale and balanced it against a feather to see if it was heavy with sin. The Egyptians worshiped many other gods, both male and female. Each deity had different forms and powers. Thousands of temples were built to these gods, and the deities were believed to live in the temples in the form of statues. Each day, the god's shrine would be opened and the statue would be dressed and given offerings of food and drink.

At the center of religious practice was the pharaoh, who was believed to be the son of the sun god Amon (also known as Re or Ra), who was represented as a male figure with a ram's head. The god of the afterlife was Osiris, who was represented as a mummy with a king's crown on its head. Anubis or Anpu, the god of the dead, was represented by a black jackal or a male figure with a dog's head. Isis was the queen of the gods, and sister-wife to Osiris. Isis was represented by a female figure wearing a headdress and seated on a throne.

An illustration from the Book of the Dead *depicts the ritual in which Osiris, the god of the afterlife, and forty-two judges weigh a dead person's heart to see if it is heavy with sin.*

constructed at Saqqara for King Djoser (also known as Zoser) around 2650 B.C. The structure, which measured about 360 by 400 feet at its base and rose to a height of nearly 200 feet, consisted of six large mastabas of diminishing size stacked one upon another.

The first true pyramid was built fifty years after Djoser's death on the sands of Meidum, about forty miles south of Memphis. The Meidum pyramid marked a drastic change in pyramid design. Workers packed the tomb's huge steps with rough-cut stones to create a slope, then encased the entire structure in limestone to give it the smooth, continuous sides of a perfect pyramid.

Egyptologists theorize that the pyramid at Meidum was built for King Sneferu, the first king of the Fourth Dynasty. They believe that Sneferu's son Khufu (Cheops in Greek), wanting to outdo his father, ordered the construction of the Great Pyramid at Giza. After the death of Khufu, his son Khafre and grandson Menkaure each built smaller pyramids at Giza.

The Egyptians also built a guard—the Great Sphinx—to stand permanent watch over Giza. King Khafre is said to have ordered the colossal statue, the face of which is believed to be Khafre's, complete with his royal headdress and traditional false beard. The body is that of a reclining lion, the mythical creature Egyptians believed guarded sacred sites.

Three hundred years or so after the completion of the Sphinx and the three pyramids at Giza, the great age of pyramid building came to an end. Pepi II was the last king to rule over a centralized government in Egypt for several centuries. He erected the final Old Kingdom pyramid at Saqqara. To recapture the glories of the past, later pharaohs revived pyramid building in the Twelfth Dynasty of the Middle Kingdom (2040–1640 B.C.). But their pyramids were smaller and made of sun-dried mud and brick rather than stone blocks. These structures eventually crumbled into mounds of rubble, worn down by the sun, wind, and occasional rains of North Africa.

The Great Sphinx, with the head of King Khafre and the body of a lion, stands guard over the Giza pyramids.

Today there may be dozens of undiscovered pyramids buried beneath the desert sands. What secrets are held in these buildings can only be imagined. For all the knowledge and understanding of the pyramids amassed in the past two centuries, much of what archaeologists believe is actually speculation, and much hard information remains hidden by the drifting sands. And as researchers learn more, old accepted theories fall by the way. As the inscrutable expression of the Sphinx warns all visitors, the mystery of the pyramids may never be known or understood by mere mortals.

Chapter 1

How Were the Pyramids Built?

The three pyramids at Giza are among the largest buildings ever constructed on earth. They were not the first pyramids ever built, however; rather, they represent the culmination and convergence of an advanced civilization's achievement in art, architecture, astronomy, language, and engineering. It was the Step Pyramid, built for Djoser during the Third Dynasty around forty-six hundred years ago at Saqqara, that marked the beginning of the glorious age of the pyramids.

Archaeologists believe that the Step Pyramid was probably designed by Djoser's official architect, Imhotep, who, in addition to acting as the designer and project foreman, was a priest known as "Chancellor and Great Seer of the Sun God Re." Imhotep's pyramid was the first building ever constructed with stone masonry—that is, stones that were cut, carved, and stacked by mathematical design, rather than rough rocks piled one upon another.

Although the exact construction methods remain a mystery, archaeologists have advanced widely accepted theories explaining the building of the Step Pyramid. During construction, which might have lasted more than thirty-four years, workers had to quarry huge blocks of limestone cut from a nearby cliff with tools of stone, copper, and wood. The rough-cut blocks then had to be moved across the shallow waters of the Nile to Saqqara.

Though the source of the building materials is easily explained, how the builders overcame a major logistical problem is not, as Mark Lehner writes in *The Complete Pyramids:*

A bronze statue of priest and architect Imhotep, who is believed to have designed the Step Pyramid at Saqqara.

Priests and Magicians

Imhotep, believed to be the architect and construction foreman of the Step Pyramid, was also a priest. On the Ancient Egyptian Culture website maintained by Minnesota State University, the role of priests and their magician colleagues is explained:

> The priesthood of ancient Egypt has a far reaching and deep history. . . . Rather than seek the divine and develop a rapport with the gods, the role of the priest was akin to an everyday job. For, as the pharaoh was seen as a god himself, the priests and priestesses were seen as stand-ins for the pharaoh; as it was the greater job of the priests and priestesses to keep Egyptian society in good order, as is the case with most theoretically based societies. . . .
>
> [Set] apart from the hierarchy of priests are the lay magicians who supplied a commoner's understanding of Egyptian religion. Through the use of magic and their connection to the gods, lay magicians provided a service to their community, usually consisting of counseling, magical arts, healing, and ceremony. Lay magicians . . . belonged to a large temple known simply as "The House of Life." Laymen would come to "The House of Life" to meet with a magician, priest or priestess to have their dreams interpreted, to supply magical spells and charms, to be healed and to counteract malevolent magic, and to supply incantations of various types. Though the House of Life provided its Laymen with many prescriptive cures for common ills, it was largely shrouded in mystery in ancient times. In fact, the library of The House of Life was shrouded in great secrecy, as it contained many sacred rites, books, and secrets of the temple itself which were thought could harm the pharaoh, the priests, and all of Egypt itself.

The average depth of the Nile flood waters was not sufficient to float huge limestone casing blocks or granite beams to the foot of the pyramid plateau. Yet there is no evidence that the Old Kingdom Egyptians cut [permanent] . . . canals . . . across the flood plain. [2]

While some researchers speculate that the builders dredged deeper channels in natural basins to float the stones on raftlike boats, there is no proof that such waterways ever were constructed.

However the workers managed to transport the stones across the Nile, the massive rocks were finally dragged to the building site by teams of men using papyrus ropes. Once at the site, the blocks were carved into finished form and hauled into place.

The Step Pyramid's Mysteries

Djoser's Step Pyramid is the oldest surviving stone structure in the world, and was, as David Roberts writes in the January 1995 *National Geographic,* the "world's first great construction project."[3] It was also a prototype for pyramids built later. The

French Egyptologist Jean-Philippe Lauer oversees excavation of the Step Pyramid in 1996.

monument, however, was buried under drifting desert sands for untold centuries. Not until 1926 was the Step Pyramid unearthed from the desert floor by French Egyptologist Jean-Philippe Lauer. Lauer spent the next sixty-eight years excavating the site, about twice as long as it actually took to build what has become known as Djoser's "Mansion of Eternity."[4]

Over the decades Lauer's workmen carefully removed the sand from around the Step Pyramid to reveal a pyramid complex that measures 1,700 by 908 feet and is surrounded by a wall nearly 35 feet high. The complex contains two shrines, one dedicated to the vulture goddess Nekhbet, the other to the snake goddess Uto. The complex also includes unexplainable structures, such as elaborate temples purposely filled with rock, and doors that lead nowhere. Roberts describes the scene and the mystery surrounding the pyramid complex:

> I was struck by the strangeness of Djoser's complex. Everything about the place bespoke illusion. Towering limestone columns had been shaped to mimic the sway and droop of leafy plants. Immovable doors hung on great carved hinges. Facades called false doors, through which the pharaoh's *ka*, or vital force, was presumed to pass, lay recessed within walls. The interiors of dummy temples were packed with rubble.

> No one knows why the Egyptians created this fantastic scene, but some archaeologists speculate that there was an Old Kingdom belief that a work of art, a building, even a chanted phrase had power and utility in the afterlife in direct proportion to its usefulness in the real world. In this view, each false door, each dummy temple "worked" in the afterlife precisely because it could not function in this one.[5]

The First True Pyramid

Djoser devoted a large percentage of his kingdom's resources to insure his success in the afterlife. But it was Sneferu, the first king of the Fourth Dynasty, who in 2575 B.C. initiated a pyramid-building boom unrivaled in history.

Sneferu's contribution to the Pyramid Age began with a seven-level step pyramid at Meidum built to resemble Djoser's. For reasons unknown—possibly because this pyramid was the work of an earlier king—Sneferu ordered the addition of another step, bringing the total number to eight. This phase of the Meidum pyramid was completed within fourteen years and the king then moved his royal headquarters to Dahshur, a site twenty-five miles north.

Although his motives remain unclear, about fifteen years later Sneferu commissioned his workmen to return to

Meidum to remake the step pyramid into a true pyramid by filling in the steps with stones and covering them with a fine white limestone casing. It is believed that during that time, advances in engineering, materials handling, and architectural techniques allowed construction with huge slabs of stone, rather than smaller blocks. The final tomb was 302 feet high, with each side stretching 473 feet.

Certain aspects of the Meidum pyramid continue to baffle Egyptologists. Perhaps the most unusual fact is that the freestanding stone monuments called stelae, located in the pyramid's chapel, never mention the name of Sneferu. This was highly unusual, as Lehner writes: "Sneferu's two stelae in the eastern chapel were never inscribed with his [name] but were left completely blank—a fact that seems inexplicable given our understanding of the Egyptian belief that, devoid of a name, a monument (like a person) would have no identity."[6]

Piles of debris and rubble are visible around the base of the collapsed pyramid at Meidum.

The pyramid at Meidum is also unique in that it has collapsed over time, and piles of rubble and debris are heaped around the base. No one has been able to determine why—or when—the pyramid collapsed. A majority of researchers have ruled out a slow disintegration over the centuries, and theorize that the building may have collapsed while still under construction, causing the builders—and the king—to abandon the project. This theory could also explain why Sneferu's name was never added to the stelae.

"The Gleaming Pyramid of the South"

Meanwhile, Sneferu ordered his workers to build two more monumental pyramids at Dahshur. The first of these structures was called the "Gleaming Pyramid of the South" by the ancient Egyptians, but is known today as the Bent Pyramid because of its unusual convex shape, known as a rhomboid in geometric terms. Egyptologists are fascinated by the style and construction of the Bent Pyramid, whose slope changes from about 52° at the base to 43.5° about two-thirds of the way to the top.

Some believe that during the construction of the Bent Pyramid, Sneferu's project at Meidum collapsed, and the builders were forced to change the angles of the Bent Pyramid to prevent a similar accident. Others think that the foundation of the pyramid was insufficient to support its weight, as a website about the Bent Pyramid states:

> The underlying sands and shales eventually proved unable to support the weight of the pyramid, the first to be designed as a true geometric pyramid and one that would have surpassed the height of the Great Pyramid had it been completed as planned. Although various theories have been proposed to explain the curious change in angle which gives the Bent Pyramid its name, the most convincing reason for its shape was the necessity to remedy the cracks and fissures caused by subsidence [settling] which began to appear even while this pyramid was being built.
>
> The original plan was to build a true pyramid with a rather steep slope of about 60 degrees, but about half-way through construction the outer casing began to crack. To prevent further subsidence, additional masonry was added to all four sides, reducing the angle of inclination to 54 degrees. Yet it was too late. Fissures in the blocks of the completed internal chambers appeared.[7]

Whether or not this theory is correct, the Bent Pyramid was finally covered with a fine finished facing. Unlike the other pyramids, which over the centuries were stripped of their facade by locals needing building material, the Bent Pyramid retains this stone.

The Great Pyramids at Giza

Sneferu was the greatest pyramid builder in history, having constructed three full-size pyramids and possibly two smaller ones that consumed more than 4.7 million cubic yards of stone. As for why Sneferu needed so many pyramids when previous kings built only one, there are few clues. Since he could only be buried in one place, and since he did not place his name on his structures, some question whether Sneferu built them at all. Others believe that the pyramids were part of an ongoing civil engineering project that was planned from start to finish before construction began.

Whatever the case, the pyramid projects continued when Sneferu's son Khufu ordered construction to begin at Giza around 2550 B.C. Here, on a plateau located on the west bank of the Nile, a building boom ensued that resulted in the Great Sphinx along with three towering structures, the Great Pyramid of Khufu and the pyramids built by his son Khafre and grandson Menkaure.

More than two thousand years after the pyramids were constructed, around 443 B.C., the ancient Greek historian Herodotus visited Egypt and wrote about the building of the Great Pyramid in his *History*. Although his accuracy has been debated, Herodotus's account was the first to actually record the events surrounding the construction of the pyramids:

> Cheops became king over [the Egyptians], and he drove them into the extremity of misery. For first he shut up all the temples, to debar them from [worshiping] in them, and thereafter he ordered all Egyptians to work for himself. To some was assigned the [job of] dragging of great stones from the stone quarries in the Arabian mountains as far as the Nile; to others he gave orders, when these stones had been taken across the river in boats, to drag them, again, as far as the Libyan hills. The people worked in gangs of one hundred thousand each for a period of three months. The

people were afflicted for ten years of time in building the road along which they dragged the stones—in my opinion a work as great as the pyramid itself. For the length of the road is more than half a mile, and its breadth is sixty feet, and its height, at its highest, is forty-eight feet. It is made of polished stone, and there are figures carved on it.[8]

Around 443 B.C., more than two thousand years after they were built, Greek historian Herodotus visited the pyramids and wrote about their construction.

Herodotus also notes that writing on the pyramid walls records the amounts of money spent on foodstuffs such as radishes, onions, and garlic for the workmen.

Modern researchers doubt the account of Herodotus, maintaining that only around twenty to thirty thousand workers built the Great Pyramids, and that workers were not slaves but rather volunteers. In fact several work groups carved their team names into the stones of the Great Pyramid, and their monikers, such as "The Pure Ones of Khufu" or "Those Who Know Unas," indicate their pride and lofty intentions. Of course one team, "The Drunks of Menkaure," seemed more intent on showing their sense of humor.

Notwithstanding the debate over the particulars of the *History,* researchers agree that it must have taken quite a large group of people to move over 2 million stone blocks into place to build Khufu's tomb. The average stone weighed around 2.5 tons, and the largest blocks weighed up to 70 tons. It has been proven that some of these rocks came from quarries located five hundred miles from Giza; to this day, no one understands how these huge rocks were transported to the pyramid site.

Researchers estimate that it took approximately thirty years to build the Great Pyramid. Egyptologists are awed by what the builders accomplished using only the most primitive tools. As Bauval and Gilbert write:

Just how [the pyramids] were built remains a mystery; even today we would be hard pressed to replicate them with all the advantages of modern technology. At the time of the Ancient Egyptians there were no dump-trucks or cranes, no steel cables or hoists, not even iron tools. Without the benefit of so much as a simple pulley, they built mountains from stone and, with a precision that is truly astonishing, laid these out on the desert floor.[9]

The Mysteries of the Great Pyramid

Throughout the centuries, observers have marveled at the remarkable features of Khufu's pyramid, which rises 481 feet above the desert floor and contains enough rock to pave an 8-foot-wide, 4-inch-deep highway from San Francisco to New York City.

The base of the Great Pyramid is nearly a perfect square, stretching 756 feet per side with a difference of less than 6 inches between the longest and shortest sides. Some attach great significance to the length of 756 feet, as noted on the Modern Mysteries website:

Each of the Pyramid's four walls, when measured as a straight line, are 9,131 inches, for a total of 36,524 inches. At first glance, this number may not seem significant, but move the decimal point over and you get 365.24. Modern science has shown us that the exact length of the solar year is 365.24 days.[10]

Although the Egyptians probably calculated the exact length of a solar year, they did not use units of measurement such as inches and feet. This theory shows how willing many people are to attach significance to seemingly irrelevant facts. The accuracy of other precise measurements found on the structure, however, is truly astonishing if only for the proof it provides of the Egyptians' advanced construction techniques.

On the face of the pyramid, the flat surface stones were cut within 1/100th of an inch of a perfectly straight line, and all cuts are at perfect 90° right angles. The stones were piled one upon another with a constant gap of 0.02 inch—thinner than a knife blade—purposely left between them; even in the twenty-first century, modern builders cannot achieve this degree of accuracy with such heavy stones.

The tiny gap between the stones was filled with a white gluelike cement that connected the stones and prevented water from seeping into the cracks. This amazing substance has remained intact for nearly forty-five centuries and has a surface hardness stronger than the limestone blocks that it joins.

In addition to this glue, other design features of the Great Pyramid guaranteed that it would last for thousands of years, according to Modern Mysteries:

> Like 20th century bridge designs, the Pyramid's corner-stones have balls and sockets built into them. Several football fields long, the Pyramid is subject to expansion and contraction movements from heat and cold, as well as earthquakes, settling, and other such phenomena. After 4,600 years its structure would have been significantly damaged without such construction. [11]

The design and position of the Great Pyramid has also been correlated mathematically with the geometry and geography of the earth. Besides being built so that two corners at the pyramid's base line up with true north on the compass, the curves of the building mimic the curvature of the earth. According to Modern Mysteries:

> All four sides of the Pyramid are very slightly and evenly bowed in, or concave. This effect, which cannot

be detected by looking at the Pyramid from the ground, was discovered around 1940 by a pilot taking aerial photos to check certain measurements. As measured by today's laser instruments, all of these perfectly cut and intentionally bowed stone blocks duplicate exactly the curvature of the earth. The radius of this bow is equal to the radius of the earth. This radius of curvature [was unknown to Western scientists until the sixteenth century A.D.].

An illustration shows how workers might have used a lever to hoist heavy stones in place during construction of the pyramids.

[In addition the] Pyramid is located at the exact center of the Earth's land mass. That is, its East-West axis corresponds to the longest land parallel across the Earth, passing through Africa, Asia, and America. Similarly, the longest land meridian on Earth, through Asia, Africa, Europa, and Antarctica, also passes right through the Pyramid. Since the Earth has enough land area to provide 3 billion possible building sites for the Pyramid, the odds of its having been built where it is are 1 in 3 billion. [12]

The scope and meaning of these and other facts about the Great Pyramid leave more questions than answers. How the stones were cut, moved, and put in place with such stunning accuracy remains a mystery. How the Egyptians measured the angles and why they picked this exact spot to build the pyramid complex is unknown. Modern scientists doubt that the Egyptians were aware of the exact curvature of the earth or the precise location of an east-west axis. Whatever the case, as Lehner writes: "In terms of its size, the technical accomplishments of its construction, the great concern for [alignment with the cardinal directions], and the organization it represents, Khufu's pyramid was a rather astonishing leap forward." [13]

Moving Stone

In sheer size, the Great Pyramid complex was a behemoth building project that required massive rocks to be precisely put into place at intervals of mere minutes for more than three decades. Lehner describes the astounding quantity of rock moved during Khufu's time in power:

Even with a reign of 30 to 32 years, the estimated combined mass of . . . [over 95 million cubic feet] for his pyramid, causeway, two temples, satellite pyramid, three [smaller] queens' pyramids and officials' mastabas [small rectangular tombs] means that Khufu's builders had to set in place a staggering . . .

The Pyramid Complex

Although they continue to dominate the skyline, the pyramids were just a few of the structures at Giza, including hundreds of other buildings believed necessary for the pharaoh to move into the afterworld.

Outside each pyramid was a mortuary temple connected to a funerary building by a long covered causeway, an amazing walkway more than 130 feet high. Researchers believe that the pharaoh's body was mummified in the first building and transported down the causeway in a full-size boat to the mortuary temple. This passage symbolized the king's passage from the physical world to the underworld. The mummy was then taken from the temple to the pyramid to be entombed. The causeway stretched past dozens of low rectangular mastabas, built from mud and brick, where the bodies of various relatives, priests, and officials were buried. At the Khufu complex were also three smaller pyramids about one-fifth the size of the Great Pyramid. These monuments are thought to have been built for Khufu's mother and later queens.

The Great Pyramid itself was surrounded by a Turah limestone wall more than twenty-six feet high, which enclosed a thirty-three-foot-wide courtyard paved with limestone bricks. This area was filled with finely carved columns, statues, and sanctuaries.

[8,122 cubic feet] of stone per day, the rate of one average-size block [of 2.5 tons] every two or three minutes in a ten-hour day. [14]

Despite this calculation, no village or city has ever been unearthed that could have accommodated the army of laborers who necessarily would have lived near the building site.

Although no one has answered the question of how these heavy stones were brought to Giza, researchers guess that they were moved into place by hundreds of men using papyrus ropes to pull them up large ramps built of mud, stone, and wood.

A constant stream of workers was needed at the site, including replacements for the hundreds who were injured or killed during construction. In the early 1990s, a graveyard with nearly six hundred tombs of those who are believed to have labored on the Great Pyramid was excavated. Examination of bodies found in the tombs reveals that the hard labor of building the pyramids took a heavy toll on the workers' bodies. According to Roberts, their "skeletons, their

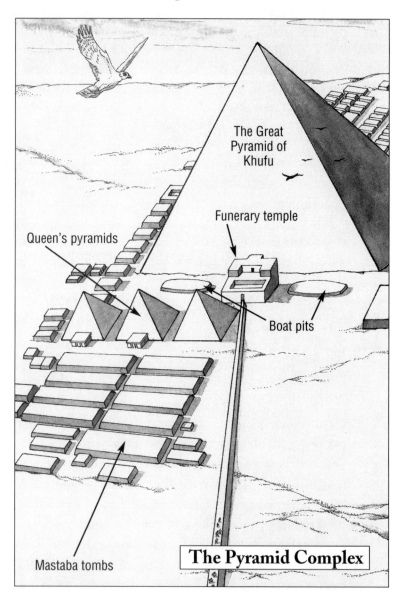

The Great Pyramid of Khufu

Funerary temple

Queen's pyramids

Boat pits

Mastaba tombs

The Pyramid Complex

vertebrae [were] compressed and damaged by years of carrying heavy loads. Some were missing fingers and even limbs."[15]

Examinations of skeletons excavated at the Great Pyramid revealed that the hard labor of building the pyramids exacted a heavy toll on the workers' bodies.

The Mysterious End of an Era

After Khufu's death, work continued on the Great Pyramid while the pharaoh's son Khafre began work on a second pyramid. At 705 feet per side that structure is slightly smaller than the Great Pyramid, and about 10 feet shorter. This slight deficiency is not obvious to observers, however, because Khafre's pyramid was built on a part of the Giza plateau that is 33 feet higher than the site of the Great Pyramid.

The third pyramid at the Giza complex was built by Menkaure, Khufu's grandson. With about 10 percent of the mass of his grandfather's Great Pyramid, Menkaure's tomb is 335 feet by 343 feet and rises to a height of around 213 feet.

It appears that work was halted on Menkaure's pyramid before it was completed, and pyramids the size of Khufu's were never attempted again. As the glorious Pyramid Age of the Fourth Dynasty drew to a close, several smaller pyramids were constructed by Fifth Dynasty pharaohs, but as Bauval and Gilbert write:

> It is obvious to anyone visiting the pyramids that after the Fourth Dynasty there was a sharp decline in the skill of pyramid building. The kings of the Fifth Dynasty built five small pyramids . . . [about five miles] southeast of Giza, and a further two small pyramids at Saqqara, not far from [Djoser's] step-pyramid. All of these were rather poorly constructed, and the workmanship of the inner core, which has mostly collapsed, is very much shoddier than that of their illustrious predecessors of the Fourth Dynasty. All the Fifth Dynasty pyramids are now major heaps of rubble, some more like mounds than pyramids. Four small pyramids were built by the Sixth Dynasty pharaohs at Saqqara, all about [173 feet] high and of even shoddier workmanship. With these last the Pyramid Age . . . came to a close. [16]

Taken together, all the pyramids built after the Fourth Dynasty used less than half the limestone used in Khufu's pyramid alone. The cause of this great decline has mystified Egyptologists for centuries. Not only were architects and engineers of the Fifth and Sixth Dynasties unable to draw on the experience of the previous pyramid builders, but the quality of the workmanship declined so rapidly that it was as if all the skilled Egyptian masons simply disappeared.

The most obvious explanation of this decline is that Egyptian society was disrupted by some sort of political upheaval. But there are few records to support such a theory. As Bauval and Gilbert write: "If the truth is told, nobody knows what happened; conventional reasoning cannot explain the evidence we have before us. All we can say is that whatever happened at the end of the Fourth Dynasty caused the eventual collapse . . . of the great Pyramid Age."[17]

Made from Concrete?

Just as experts debate the reason for the end of the Pyramid Age, speculation about how the monuments were built continues. One observer, at least, challenges the notion that the stones were cut from cliffs and carried into place:

> The carving and hoisting theory . . . raises questions that have been insufficiently answered. Using stone and copper tools, how did workers manage to make the pyramid faces absolutely flat? How did they make the faces meet at a perfect point at the summit? How did they make the tiers so level? How could the required amount of workers maneuver on the building site? How did they make the blocks so uniform? How were some of the heaviest blocks in the pyramid placed at great heights? How were twenty-two acres of casing blocks all made to fit to a hair's breadth and closer? How was all of the work done in about [thirty] years? Experts can only guess. And Egyptologists must admit that the problems have not been resolved.[18]

In the early 1980s, while searching for answers to these questions, Professor Joseph Davidovits devised a theory that the pyramids were constructed from a type of concrete known as agglomerated limestone, rather than from blocks of quarried stone. To do so, builders would have pulverized the nearby soft limestone cliffs and carried the fine particulate to the building site where it was mixed with water, lime, clay, and salt to form a concretelike substance. This thick liquid was then poured into wooden, stone, clay, or brick molds that were already in place on the structure. After drying, the molds were removed, leaving the hard blocks in place. Davidovits believes that such an endeavor would have only required hundreds of workers, rather than tens of thousands, as estimated by many traditional Egyptologists.

Davidovits supports his theory by pointing out that Egyptian artists were making extremely hard stone vases in this manner at the time the pyramids were constructed.

While this hypothesis seems to make sense, many Egyptologists vehemently deny its validity on the basis of the existence of blocks at Giza that have fossils clearly embedded in them, proving that they are solid rock, not a concrete aggregate.

The fact that theories continue to be put forth four and a half thousand years after the pyramids were constructed is a testimony to the skill and knowledge of the ancient Egyptians who built them. Perhaps Lehner states it best on the "This Old Pyramid" website:

> There's something about the pyramids here at Giza that inspires people to be very passionate about all kinds of different theories about what they hide, how they were built, what they mean. I have maps showing [imagined] whole subway systems underneath the Giza plateau, hidden chambers and tunnels, great charts of circles and intersecting lines showing the mathematical relationships of these pyramids to each other, to the Sphinx, to the stars, to Bethlehem, to Manhattan. There are just files and files and files of these ideas. But the bottom line on all these ideas, including those of Egyptologists, is that they have to stand the test of bedrock reality.[19]

Chapter 2

The Inner Chambers

The mysterious and imposing outline of the pyramids towering over the desert has attracted tourists and scholars for thousands of years. But while the impressive exteriors of the pyramids remain a source of mystery and wonder, it is the meaning and purpose of the interior spaces that are subject to the most intense speculation.

Djoser's Step Pyramid in Saqqara, probably used as a prototype by the ancient Egyptians for later pyramids, contains three standard features that would be found on later pyramids, according to Lehner: "the descending corridor; central shaft with the granite vault; and [a replica of] the king's palace with its blue-tiled chambers."[20] The pyramid also contains more than 3.5 miles of tunnels, shafts, chambers, and galleries that twist and turn beneath the complex.

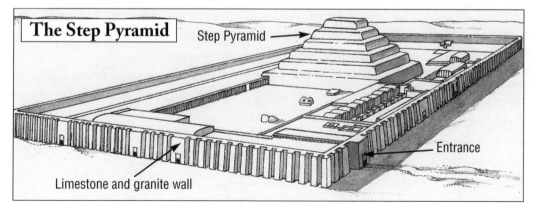

The Step Pyramid

Step Pyramid

Entrance

Limestone and granite wall

The room that is believed to be Djoser's burial vault is located at the end of a 23-foot-square central shaft that plunges 92 feet below ground. The burial vault at the end of the shaft is about 9 feet by 6 feet, and is 5 feet high. The ceiling is decorated with large five-point stars. Lehner suggests the significance of these stars:

> This motif, one that the Egyptians placed over royal tomb chambers for centuries, embodies one of the paradoxes of the pyramids. Djoser may lie after death underground, under millions of tons of masonry, but the roof of the chamber is 'open' to the night sky, to which his soul is free to fly.[21]

The burial vault has only one entrance, which was filled by a 3.5-ton plug of granite after the pharaoh's body was—theoretically—placed in the chamber. Then the open spaces surrounding the vault were filled in with dirt and debris.

Djoser's Mysteries

Although the chamber was meant to hold the mummified remains of Djoser, and sealed from intruders by tons of rock, experts are uncertain as to whether the pharaoh was actually entombed there. The only human remains found in the royal burial chamber were a mummified foot that radiocarbon dating shows was placed there about five hundred years after Djoser's death. The pharaoh's body has never been found.

There are many other mysteries concerning Djoser's Step Pyramid. Archaeologists have discovered the hipbone of an approximately eighteen-year-old woman in one of the finished rooms inside the pyramid, but radiocarbon dating indicates that this woman died hundreds of years before Djoser's reign. Other galleries are filled with roughly forty thousand pieces of plates and cups made of valuable stone such as alabaster. These, too, appear to have been made in the centuries before Djoser was born. Because of the royal inscriptions on them, Lehner speculates that the dishes might have belonged to

Making a Mummy

The pyramids contained the mummified corpses of Egyptian kings. The National Geographic website "How to Make a Mummy" explains the extraordinarily successful process of preserving the dead:

It was startling. More than 5,000 years ago, after burying their dead, the ancient Egyptians learned that the burning desert sands desiccated corpses. Instead of turning to dust, the skin shriveled up and clung to the bones. Mummification—the practice of dressing for success, eternal success—had begun.

And since they didn't want to spend eternity looking rotten, those who could afford to had their bodies painstakingly embalmed. Embalming, as practiced in ancient Egypt, was a lost art, until [recently].

Wielding a tool much like a crochet hook, the ancient embalmers emptied the skull by pulling clumps of brain matter out through the nostrils.

Delicate and skilled, they caused no damage to the visage of their dearly departed. Slicing the smallest possible incision into the abdomen, embalmers plucked out the stomach, liver, intestines, and other organs. Beautifully sculpted canopic jars stored the cured entrails for all eternity.

Natron, a type of salt, was the embalmers' secret weapon. It coaxed moisture from the flesh and reduced odors. Small packets were stuffed inside the abdominal cavity. The body was covered with some 400 pounds of it. Thirty-five days . . . [later they] anointed the body, by now dehydrated, with frankincense and myrrh.

Then the wrapping started—layer after layer of linen, decorated with hieroglyphic prayers. A small amulet was placed over the only organ left inside, the heart.

With a final benediction, the mummy embarked on its journey to the afterworld and eternal life: "You are young again. You live again. You are young again. You live again. Forever" [ancient Egyptian prayer for the dead].

Djoser's ancestors, and were taken, along with the bones of the woman, from other burial sites in the area. Who might have done this, why, and when are all mysteries.

There is another, unfinished burial chamber beneath the pyramid, this one decorated with alabaster and other costly stone. Why this elaborate chamber was built, only to be left empty, is unknown.

The purpose of many of the interior spaces of the pyramid is also mysterious. Underground passageways connect elaborately decorated rooms that might have resembled rooms in Djoser's palace. Other rooms were never completed and appear to have been abandoned, possibly because Djoser died before construction was finished.

Djoser's complex also contains a chamber known as the South Tomb that is underground but not under the pyramid. Though it is constructed of granite much like the vault in the Step Pyramid, it is too small in size to hold the king's body. Lehner raises many questions about this tiny room:

> What was placed in this vault, too small for human burial? Various suggestions have been made: that it was a fictive tomb for a ritual death during [a special ceremony] when the king renewed his vital forces; that it was the home of the king's *ka;* that it was the burial place of the royal placenta, preserved from birth until death; that it was for the burial of the crowns; or that . . . it might have been for the king's internal organs, removed during mummification. [22]

The Mysterious Mummy of Meidum

While the meaning of the tiny room at Djoser's pyramid is open to speculation, the question, Why was the pharaoh's mummified corpse never found? might have been answered at Sneferu's pyramid at Meidum.

Deep within the Meidum pyramid, a small, crudely built chamber contains neither a stone coffin known as a sarcophagus nor any mummified remains. In a nearby flat-topped mastaba, however, which can only be entered by an ancient tunnel dug by robbers, a large T-shaped chamber contains a huge sarcophagus carved out of red granite that was quarried five hundred miles away. Lehner speculates that Sneferu's massive pyramid was only a symbolic tomb, and his body was actually buried in a simple mud-walled mastaba within the pyramid complex. Roberts comments on this theory:

> Here, if Lehner's hunch proves correct, was the Old Kingdom principle of illusion as a higher truth at its most stunning. The pyramid itself—at least in the case of [Meidum]—might be a pseudo-tomb, made somehow more powerful in the afterlife of the pharaoh who only pretended to be buried there. [23]

Possibly, this was a trick that Djoser had used and Sneferu adopted as well. Although Sneferu's sarcophagus was pillaged by grave robbers dozens of centuries ago, the mummy that might have been Sneferu was still within the mastaba in 1901, when Egyptologist W. M. Flinders Petrie became the first archaeologist to enter the tomb. The mummy had been prepared in the most careful and elaborate manner, with linen wrapped around each bone and joint, and eye sockets filled with balls of paste. The remains were shipped to the British Museum in London, but there they were inexplicably lost. As a consequence, the

A stone statue of Djoser, the Third Dynasty king who commissioned construction of the Step Pyramid.

mystery of the mummy at the Meidum mastaba has yet to be resolved.

Inside Khufu's Tomb

Like his father before him, the location of Khufu's body remains a mystery. Ironically, the only existing image of the builder of the world's largest pyramid is a tiny statue—only three inches high—of Khufu sitting on a little throne. And while what they know of ancient Egyptian religious beliefs would lead researchers to think that there should be great treasures inside the Great Pyramid, no such riches have ever been found. This fact, however, has not stopped robbers over the years from attempting to loot the pyramids.

The first recorded entrance into the Great Pyramid was by a team of robbers looking for the wealth rumored to lie within. In A.D. 820, Caliph Al Mamoun searched the face of the Great Pyramid looking for the secret door he assumed was constructed by the builders. Finding no such entrance, the

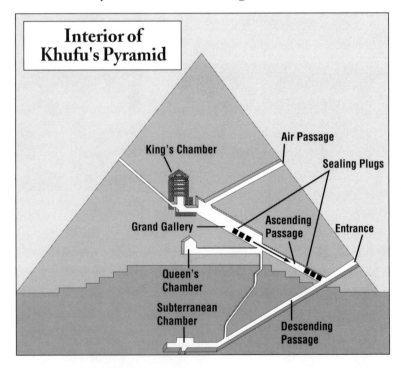

Interior of Khufu's Pyramid

King's Chamber

Air Passage

Sealing Plugs

Grand Gallery

Ascending Passage

Entrance

Queen's Chamber

Subterranean Chamber

Descending Passage

caliph and his team simply began to dig a tunnel into the pyramid's north face. After weeks of futile digging, the men had tunneled only about 107 feet. Their luck changed, however, when they heard a large stone fall within the pyramid. By tunneling about 10 feet in the direction of the sound, they broke through into a narrow sloping corridor, now known as the Descending Passage, which led to the original hidden entrance 24 feet east of the center axis.

The caliph and his men walked down this passage, less than four feet high and four feet wide, into the center of the pyramid. After sloping down through the pyramid's building blocks at a steep 26° angle for 92.5 feet, the passage continues through the bedrock for another 99 feet. Like the outer construction of the pyramid, this passage was built with incredible precision—deviating less than 3/8 inch from a straight line over the course of nearly 200 feet, half of it through solid rock. Moreover, it follows an exact north-south course.

The Descending Passage ends at an empty roughly hewn pit, known now as the Subterranean Chamber, 100 feet beneath the ground. This room, about 46 by 23 feet and 17 feet high, appears to have been left unfinished. Some have speculated that this chamber was meant to be the final resting place for Khufu, but was abandoned while the pyramid was still under construction. This theory has been discounted, however, as illogical: The builders, it would seem, would not have changed their minds about the final resting place of the king once the pyramid was already under construction.

The chamber has some mysterious features, such as a tunnel, only wide enough to hold a single person, that leads from the Subterranean Chamber to a dead end. Why a man would struggle to chip this tunnel to nowhere out of solid stone remains a mystery, but Egyptologists take it as proof that the Subterranean Chamber was not meant to be the pharaoh's final resting place because in no other pyramids can other rooms be accessed from the King's Chamber. Furthermore, the Descending Passage is too narrow to have accommodated the sarcophagus of a king as renowned as Khufu.

Passages and Galleries

These conundrums were not, we may assume, on the minds of the caliph's men, who were searching for gold and treasure, and who must have been bitterly disappointed with the results of their search. On the way back up the Descending Passage, the workmen noticed a granite plug in the ceiling. This plug filled an opening that led to the so-called Ascending Passage upward into the heart of the Great Pyramid. On the way up several more granite plugs impeded their progress. Instead of moving the plugs, the men dug into the softer limestone surrounding them and continued on.

Finally the caliph and his men came to another empty room, which they called the Queen's Chamber, although later archaeologists have concluded that the room was never meant for the queen. Instead the room, about half the length of the Subterranean Chamber—and centered exactly between the north and south sides of the pyramid—was probably meant to hold a statue that represented Khufu's *ka*. Again the caliph's men found no reward for their work.

They had been working at a backbreaking angle in the steep tunnels, but they found an open place at the junction of the Ascending and Descending passages that led to a high-roofed hallway now known as the Grand Gallery, described by Bauval and Gilbert:

> Running from the level of the Queen's Chamber up to that of the King's Chamber is the amazing architectural creation known as the Grand Gallery. This is in many ways the most elaborate and mysterious feature of a whole internal system of the Great Pyramid, and words can scarcely do it justice. It runs upward at the same angle as the ascending corridor but instead of being a narrow, crouched tunnel it is [26 feet] high. When you are inside, it gives the impression of being even higher as it sweeps towards the King's Chambers at the top end. It is a very curious structure indeed, for

though it looks rather like a massive staircase, there are no steps as such. Yet it appears highly functional and was carefully finished in finely smoothed Tura limestone.

Although the Grand Gallery is now easier to explore, it is still overwhelmingly mysterious . . . as with so much Egyptian architecture, it looks so ancient that it seems almost modern. There is a quasi-inhuman quality about the Grand Gallery that is hard to

Steps and a railing have been added to make it easier to navigate the Grand Gallery, the ascending hallway that leads to the King's Chamber in the Great Pyramid.

explain, as though it were not intended for people to walk up and down but to serve some other specialised or specific function. Many have remarked that the Grand Gallery looks like part of a machine, whose function is beyond us.[24]

The King's Chamber

The King's Chamber lies at the top of the Grand Gallery. The workmanship in this red granite room is amazing. With dimensions measuring exactly 34 by 17 feet, the room is a perfect double square. Although this 2-to-1 dimension is accurate within a sixteenth of an inch, no one knows the meaning behind these dimensions.

The ceiling of the King's Chamber is nineteen feet high and is finished with solid granite stones that weigh up to thirty tons each. They are perfectly smooth and so tightly joined—like the pyramid's facing stones—that the blade of a knife would not fit in the cracks between them. In addition, the

The incredible workmanship that was required to build the granite King's Chamber has astonished researchers.

width of the ceiling is the greatest distance ever spanned by the pyramid builders with solid blocks without the use of pillars for support.

At one end of the King's Chamber lies a large sarcophagus known as the Granite Coffer, which was obviously in place before the pyramid was finished because it is too large to have been moved through the structure's narrow passageways. The coffer is an engineering miracle in itself. Like the chamber, it is cut to precise 2-to-1 dimensions and hollowed out from a single block of solid red granite. No one has been able to explain how the Egyptians cut this incredibly hard stone with the primitive tools they had available. Some have speculated that they used bronze saws with diamond teeth, but even if such a tool existed, several tons of pressure would have been required in its application to cut the stone. And under such pressure, the diamond teeth would have cut into the bronze saw itself, leaving the granite unscathed. Only modern tools such as tubular drills could accomplish this task today.

In any case, there is little evidence that this finely constructed coffer ever held Khufu's mummified body. As Bauval and Gilbert write:

> Although it is believed that this was the final resting-place of Khufu, there is not the slightest evidence of a corpse having been in that chamber, not a sign of embalming material or fragment of any [artifact]. No clue, however minuscule, has ever been found in this chamber or anywhere else in the Great Pyramid. This has led many to suppose that we have not yet found the burial chamber of Khufu. [25]

The empty coffers, blank walls, and vacant rooms of the Great Pyramid have puzzled all who have pondered their meaning. Researchers have questioned if there ever was a great treasure of Khufu. While the answer might be that the tomb was plundered not long after it was constructed, the granite plugs continued to block the passageways at the time of the caliph's arrival more than thirty-three centuries later. How thieves could have entered and escaped from the King's Chamber therefore remains a mystery.

Some have speculated that the Great Pyramid might still contain other passages and chambers that have never been discovered, and that the king's architects have managed to outsmart thieves—and modern researchers—until this very day, and that Khufu's treasures are contained within these still-hidden chambers.

Giza's Other Pyramids

The next pyramids built at Giza, those of the pharaohs Khafre and Menkaure, have interior features similar to those of the Great Pyramid, though less elaborate. Like Khufu's monument, the inner chambers are remarkably devoid of writing or objects that would reveal anything about the original contents. A wooden coffin was found within Menkaure's pyramid with the pharaoh's name inscribed on it, but, mysteriously, radiocarbon dating indicates that this object was constructed centuries after the pyramids were built. Moreover, human remains found within also date to the earliest centuries of the first millennium A.D.

The most interesting objects found at the site were not in the pyramid at all. These were pieces of a large statue of Menkaure located within his mortuary temple. Lehner describes the statue and the meaning behind it:

> Among the finds in the mortuary temple were fragments of royal statues. These included the head, chest, lap, knees and shins of a larger-than-life alabaster statue of Menkaure that must have been the centrepiece of his entire complex. . . . From [where it stood], the king looked across the open court, through the entrance hall, and down the line of the causeway to the land of the living. Behind the great statue, on the other side of the back wall of the mortuary temple, at the base of the pyramid, there was probably a false door.

The statue represented the king emerging through the false door, symbolic portal to and from the underworld of the pyramid. There he received the offerings brought to him as head of his household for eternity and projected his divine force through the pyramid complex and out into the Nile Valley for the good of all Egypt.[26]

The Queen's Boudoir

Researchers consider the inner chambers of the Great Pyramid a treasure trove of scholarly information. But robbers have found little of monetary worth there. One of the three small Queen's Pyramids built next to Khufu's monument, however, has yielded amazing artifacts such as furniture and pottery, as described by Mark Lehner in *The Complete Pyramids:*

> Aligned with the . . . pyramid on the north is the deep shaft belonging to Queen Hetepheres. . . .
>
> At the very bottom of the shaft was a chamber, where the excavators found a beautiful alabaster sarcophagus and . . . a small alabaster box with the string around it still in place and its sealing intact. This was the canopic chest for the queen's internal organs.
>
> From the moment of discovery, however, it was apparent that this assemblage was a reburial, since the pottery was smashed and linen lay disintegrated among the remains of the boxes that had once contained it. Pieces of furniture that had been jammed into the chamber could be reconstructed from surviving gold foil although most of the wood had deteriorated. On top of the sarcophagus were beautiful long poles belonging to a canopy in the form of early papyrus bud columns. This canopy, if reassembled, would fit exactly into the chambers of the queen's pyramids. There were also the parts of two sitting chairs, a carrying chair, a tube for walking sticks, a headrest and two sets of silver bracelets. What we have here is the private boudoir of a queen.
>
> The first name found in the tomb was that of Sneferu. But then other texts came to light that contained the name Hetepheres. She was called 'Mother of the King' and 'Daughter of the God' and it became evident that she was the wife of Sneferu and mother of a reigning king. . . . It is not certain that Hetepheres was the mother of Khufu, who survived three older brothers.

Amazing Artwork

The pyramids of Khufu, Khafre, and Menkaure represent the height of ancient Egypt's building technology. The pyramids of the Fifth and Sixth Dynasties, constructed after those at Giza, were so poorly made that many simply crumbled into ruin over the years. Ironically, these smaller, shoddier pyramids, which did not withstand the ravages of time, have revealed much more information about the ancient Egyptians than the great monuments at Giza.

Near Saqqara, the Fifth Dynasty pyramid of the pharaoh Sahure, built around 2458 B.C., was the first to be adorned with reliefs, a type of sculpture in which shapes are cut from the surrounding stone so that figures stand out slightly against a flat background.

Unlike the Giza pyramids, Pharoah Sahure's pyramid was poorly constructed and is now little more than piles of rubble.

The reliefs at Sahure's pyramid complex show the pharaoh boldly slaying his enemies and walking on their bodies while his two sons and wife watch adoringly. In *The Pyramids of Egypt,* I. E. S. Edwards describes artwork in a nearby temple: "The reliefs in this hall . . . show the king, in the form of either a sphinx or a griffin, trampling underfoot Asiatics and Libyans [enemies of Egypt], who were led to him bound as captives by the gods."[27]

Researchers believe that artwork such as that found in Sahure's pyramid complex was created for specific reasons, as Charles Freeman explains in *The Legacy of Ancient Egypt:*

> All Egyptian art reflected the overriding desire to create and preserve the ideal order brought into being at the beginning of creation. . . . Tombs—including the pyramids of the Old Kingdom—helped the king reach his rightful place in heaven. . . . Sculptures and paintings, similarly, were placed in the tombs of kings . . . not as frivolous decoration but to create the possibility of an afterlife for the deceased, whose mummified body lay within those walls.
>
> Art was rarely just decoration or simple representation of nature. . . . The images produced through art could be brought alive. The sculpture of a man, placed in his tomb and with the correct rituals enacted over it, was thought to provide a permanent, undecaying abode for his soul after death. A painting of food could magically become the actual food itself; the column of the temple heavy with leaves could be a forest, or even the very first forest that sprang up the moment of creation. Similarly, negative images could become very powerful. A hippopotamus or snake, which might pose a threat in life, to be equally threatening after death. Artists tried to avoid depicting such negative figures altogether, in hieroglyphs as well as in painting sculpture. Where they could not be avoided, they were often neutralized by being shown in mutilated form, such as a hippopotamus with a harpoon in its side.[28]

Pharaohs who followed Sahure continued to line their pyramid complexes with reliefs and fill them with statuary. As with their predecessors, these pharaohs were surrounded by reliefs of mystical scenes and items they wanted to accompany them into the afterlife. Some were odd, such as scenes of famine with dozens of people depicted in the last stages of starvation with their withered bodies reduced to skin and bone. We might presume that the pharaoh who commissioned this work hoped that the people depicted—no doubt his enemies—would continue to starve for eternity.

The Pyramid Texts

The last pharaoh of the Fifth Dynasty was Unas (or Unis), who reigned for more than thirty years, from 2356 to 2323 B.C. During this time, he ordered the construction of a pyramid near Djoser's Step Pyramid. The burial chamber in Unas's pyramid was probably plundered in ancient times, and was not rediscovered until 1881, after a local Egyptian workman followed a jackal into a narrow hole in the ground and discovered a passage that led to the pharaoh's resting place. The workman notified the director of the Egyptian Antiquities Service and the surrounding rubble was removed and the burial chamber entered for the first time in centuries.

What the researchers found was astounding—the stone walls, passages, and columns were covered with hieroglyphic writing. Known today as Pyramid Texts, these are the world's oldest known religious writings. These pictographs represent odes to the gods and hundreds of magical spells meant to ward off evil spirits and ensure happiness in the afterlife. For example, some of the hieroglyphs express the pharaoh's desire to have an ample quantity of food and drink in the next world. And like the reliefs and statuary found in earlier pyramids, the hieroglyphs had mystical significance. As Edwards explains: "So powerful was the magic of the written word that its presence alone provided a sufficient guarantee that the thoughts expressed would be realized."[29]

The Life of a Pharaoh

In *The Pyramids of Egypt* British archaeologist I. E. S. Edwards describes the artwork carved in relief on the walls of Sahure's mortuary temple:

[In one] scene live animals, taken as booty, are shown; their number is given in the accompanying inscriptions as 123,440 head of cattle, 223,400 asses, 232,413 deer, and 243,688 sheep, but only the smallest fraction of this vast total is actually represented. . . .

On the northern side [of a wide corridor] were scenes of the king harpooning fish and fowling with a throw-stick. On the southern side, in a relief measuring about 30 feet in length, the king is shown hunting. Behind him stand his successor Neferirkake and a group of courtiers. In front are antelopes, gazelles, deer and other horned animals, driven by beaters into a large enclosure where the king shoots them with arrows from his bow. Hounds seize some of the wounded beasts by the throat and dispatch them. Here and there the sculptor has varied the regularity of the scene with such lively touches as a jerboa [small rodent] and a hedgehog about to disappear into their holes and a hyena seizing a wounded antelope as its private quarry. . . .

North of the door leading from the open court, the king, accompanied by his courtiers, was represented witnessing the departure of twelve seagoing ships to a land which is not specified, but which was probably Palestine or Syria. In the corresponding position on the south side of the door, the king and his retinue watched the return of the ships laden with cargo and carrying a number of Asiatics. Nothing in their appearance suggests that the Asiatics were prisoners; the ships may therefore have been employed on a commercial or perhaps a diplomatic errand.

The writing in Unas's pyramid describes his journey to the afterlife, as described by Michael Birrell on the "Pyramid Texts" website:

The After-life which is envisaged in the Pyramid Texts was a celestial one, containing vestiges of early . . . beliefs mixed with the new . . . concepts of the Late Old Kingdom. The tone of the texts is often threatening, and the king must bully the gods into allowing him entry into heaven. To reach Paradise, the king had to be ferried across the so-called 'Lily Lake' by a boatman called 'He-who-looks-behind-himself'. To convince the ferryman to take him across, the king used different stratagems: he could say that he was bringing the sun-god something which he needed; he could pretend that the sun-god required him to perform a task, or he could use magic to force the ferryman to take him across. If all this failed he could plead with the sun-god to instruct the ferryman to grant him passage. The king is then greeted at the gates of the Other World where heralds await to announce his arrival. Spell 518 reads "This king Pepi found the gods standing, wrapped in their garments, their white sandals on their feet. They cast off their white sandals to the earth; they threw off their garments and say 'Our heart was not glad until thy coming'."[30]

The pictographs related Unas's desire, after arriving in the afterlife, to act as a personal secretary to the sun god Re, that is, writing down his edicts and organizing his documents. In these depictions, every day Unas accompanies Re as he rows his boat, representing the sun, from east to west across the sky. At night the pair returns, rowing west to east.

Controversy over the Pyramid Texts

The 714 individual magic spells found in Unas's Pyramid Texts have been closely studied by several generations of Egyptologists since they were first discovered in the late nineteenth century. Like almost every other facet of the pyramids, the texts have provoked controversy.

Even their discovery by a workman following a jackal has a mystical quality, since the doglike animals were worshiped by the ancient Egyptians as Anubis, the god of mummification, the necropolis, and guardian of the dead on their path through the underworld.

Following the jackal's path into the burial chamber of Unas, French archaeologist Gaston Maspero was the first researcher to enter the pyramid on February 28, 1881. Working feverishly for five days, Maspero copied the images from the walls, columns, and ceiling, and rushed an interpretation into print in a research journal, writing:

> I cannot hide the fact that this tentative translation was rather rash, and I perhaps should have waited longer; I none the less thought that Egyptologists would be more grateful to me for a quick publication rather than waiting for in-depth study, and would therefore forgive me the errors in interpretation in favour of the importance of the texts. [31]

Maspero was right in believing that the Pyramid Texts would be significant. Dozens of other researchers would base their interpretations of the writings on his work over the next century and beyond. While the Pyramid Texts were pored over by generations of Egyptologists, dozens of books and articles have been published as to their meaning and interpretation.

While some have claimed that these works in earlier versions provided inspiration for the building of the pyramids, others have said that the magic and spells on the walls were nothing but expressions of the ignorant notions of a pagan culture. According to Bauval and Gilbert, those who deny their significance have reduced "the Pyramid Texts to the mumbo-jumbo of archaic and superstitious magician-priests with weird ideas about the afterlife problems of their dead kings. Hardly a religion at all, put in those terms." [32]

Despite varying interpretations, the texts remain a detailed reading of the king's journey into the afterlife and his planned deeds once there. They also provide a description of the afterworld along with myths, spells, and stories that have layers of meaning that may never be fully understood. Researchers have discovered that the order in which the spells are written on the wall are meant to be read by the *ka* of Unas himself as it rises from his mummified body and walks from the sarcophagus, along the corridor, into the antechamber next door, and out to the sky.

Why this interest in decorating suddenly appeared in a shoddily constructed pyramid while the walls of the pyramids at Giza are blank is just one mystery surrounding the inner chambers of the pyramids. With so many theories and so few answers, it may be that only the pharaoh's *ka*, floating through the afterlife, knows the secrets of the ancient dead.

Chapter 3

The Pyramids and the Stars

When the Great Pyramid at Giza was completed, it was covered with 144,000 highly polished casing stones that reflected sunlight so brightly that the pyramid could have been seen from the moon. Dozens of theories, advanced over centuries, connect the pyramids to the moon, the planets, the distant stars of the Milky Way, and even extraterrestrials. While some of these theories defy belief, there is little doubt that whoever built the pyramids had a strong bond to the sun and stars.

It is well known that the Egyptians worshiped the sun in the form of the deity Re. And most modern researchers agree that, at the very least, the pyramid shape was likely modeled on the "angels' ladders" made when the sun's rays break through the clouds. And the form may have spiritual purposes as well, according to Bauval and Gilbert: "[The] pyramid shape is essentially a solar symbol . . . it represents rays of the sun coming down to earth through the clouds. Thus the pyramid symbolizes a crude stone ramp leading the [spirit of the] pharaoh home to the sun."[33]

The importance to the ancient Egyptians of the sun and the pyramid shape is evident in this small pyramid containing an image of the sun god Re.

Modeled on Sun Rays

Researchers have yet to determine why the ancient Egyptians were so fascinated with the pyramid shape. Some believe that the monuments were modeled on the shape that sun rays make when shining through breaks in the clouds. This form was symbolized in a small pyramid-shaped stone known as a benben that represents the sun god Re and also caps the top of each pyramid. Respected Egyptologist I. E. S. Edwards of the British Museum explains this concept in *The Pyramids of Egypt:*

> [What] did the *benben* and its architectural derivative, the true pyramid, represent? Only one answer suggests itself: the rays of the sun shining down on earth. A remarkable spectacle may sometimes be seen in the late afternoon of a cloudy winter day at Giza. When standing on the road to Saqqara and gazing westwards at the pyramid plateau, it is possible to see the sun's rays striking downwards through a gap in the clouds at about the same angle as the slope of the Great Pyramid. The impression made on the mind by the scene is that the [cosmic] prototype and the [stone] replica are here ranged side by side.

Even at the time of the Step Pyramid, constructed for King Djoser around 2650 B.C., researchers suggest that the monuments were meant to be a sort of launching pad to the stars for use by the immortal souls of the pharaohs. The steps of the structure itself were believed by the Egyptians to be ladders leading to the sky. And the sarcophagus that contained a statue of the king had eyeholes, so that his icon could aid his soul's journey to the stars. Roberts writes of a conversation with French Egyptologist Jean-Philippe Lauer concerning this theory:

> On the north side of the pyramid [Lauer and I] paused before a small stone cubicle, [angled] towards the north, with a pair of tiny holes in its facade. Lauer said, "Look inside." I peered through one of the holes and was startled to see two eyes returning my stare, the blank gaze of a life-sized statue of Djoser sitting on the throne. . . .

Lauer smiled, "Of course the holes are not for you to look in but for the pharaoh to look out—perhaps at the stars in the northern sky called the Imperishables because they never set." Here, once again, was the Old Kingdom obsession with immortality in the sky. A mere statue of the pharaoh staring at the stars aided his flight to the heavens.[34]

Sundials and Observatories

Aside from the role the pyramids might have played in the pharaoh's journey to the afterlife, these structures were likely significant scientific instruments in their own right. For example, the Great Pyramid at Giza acts as a huge sundial, announcing the advent of the vernal equinox—the first day of spring, around March 21—when the earth's position makes night and day the exact same length. As Peter Tompkins explains in *Secrets of the Great Pyramid:* "In . . . spring, when the sun rises just high enough above the apex of the Great Pyramid, the whole shadow on the north face vanishes at the stroke of noon."[35]

But the Great Pyramid is more than a massive clock that can announce the arrival of spring. As far back as A.D. 450, the Roman author Proclus suggested that the pyramid was

It is believed that the Great Pyramid acted as a massive sundial that announced the arrival of spring.

not built to hold the mummified body of Khufu but was instead an astronomical observatory designed to be used to study the stars even *before* construction was completed.

This theory was revived in the nineteenth century by astronomer Richard Proctor. According to Tompkins:

> Procter theorized that the Pyramid would have made an excellent observatory at the time [that construction] had reached the summit of the Grand Gallery, which would have given onto a large square platform where the priests could observe and record the movements of the heavenly bodies. [36]

The idea that the Great Pyramid served as an observatory helps explain how some of the structures within the pyramid were so accurately located. For example, Proctor discovered that the angle of Alpha Draconis, or the North Star, in relation to points on earth might have been used as a fixed measurement on which construction of the pyramid was based. Proctor's theory states that before the pyramids were built, astronomers deduced the angle made by the North Star and the horizon and the building site was a little more than 26°. They then began digging the Descending Passage into the ground at precisely that angle. Then, as the Descending Passage was dug, the builders would have always been able to see the North Star.

Proctor then concluded that by following the angle of the star, the pyramid builders were able to construct the entire Descending Passage to the heart of the pyramid with incredible accuracy. Then, as Tompkins explains: "Once the ancients had measured the length of the Descending Passage and its angle of descent, it would have been simple, by elementary trigonometry, to locate the central spot immediately above the end of the Descending Passage as a center for the proposed pyramid." [37]

As the pyramid rose in height, and the star disappeared, troughs of water were said to have been used as mirrors to reflect the position of the North Star so that the Ascending Passage and the Grand Gallery could have been built with equal precision.

An ancient relief depicts people offering sacrifices as they reach toward the heavens. The Egyptians worshiped the sun and regarded the stars as living deities.

Although this computation seems complicated, there was a direct purpose for this building method: As the long, narrow Grand Gallery was constructed, astronomers could have watched the transits, or passages of various stars and planets, through the narrow slit in the roof. As Tompkins writes:

> Looking up through such a slot, an observer could watch the passage of the entire panoply of the zodiac, easily noting the transit of each star across a perfect meridian—precisely what is done today by the modern astronomer. . . . As Procter points out, such a Grand Gallery might well be described as the *only* very accurate method available for preparing an accurate map of the sky and of the [zodiac] . . . before the invention of the telescope in the seventeenth century of our era. . . .

> Procter surmises that someone in either the Queen's Chamber or on a flat platform . . . above the Grand Gallery could keep time by hourglass or water clock in coordination with the observers in the Gallery, who would signal the beginning or end of transit across the Gallery's field of view.[38]

Whether or not the Grand Gallery functioned as the world's first observatory, the stars were regarded as living deities by ancient Egyptians. As such, by using the light of the stars to guide the pyramid's construction, they literally would have believed that they were being instructed by the gods.

The Mysterious Air Shafts

Egyptologists at least have plausible theories for how the Grand Gallery might have been used, but other of the pyramid's structures are more resistant to explanation. The Grand Gallery leads to the King's Chamber, and from that room, two air shafts, nearly 8 inches square, extend to the outside of the pyramid ending about 262 feet above the ground. One shaft runs precisely north and the other due south. The purpose of

The Story of Osiris

Osiris, represented by the constellation now known as Orion, was one of the most important gods in ancient Egypt, as the website "Osiris, God of the Underworld and Vegetation" explains:

[Osiris is one] of the so-called "dying gods", he was the focus of a famous legend in which he was killed by the rival god [his brother] Seth. At a banquet of the gods, Seth fooled Osiris into stepping into a coffin, which he promptly slammed shut and cast into the Nile. The coffin was born by the Nile to the delta town of Byblos, where it became enclosed in a tamarisk tree. Isis, the wife of Osiris, discovered the coffin and brought it back. . . .

Seth took advantage of Isis's temporary absence on one occasion, cut the body to pieces, and cast them into the Nile. . . . Isis searched the land for the body parts of Osiris, and was eventual-

ly able to piece together his body. . . . In some Egyptian texts, the scattering of the body parts is likened to the scattering of grain in the fields, a reference to Osiris's role as a vegetation god. 'Osiris gardens'—wood-framed barley seedbeds in the shape of the god, were sometimes placed in tombs—and the plants which sprouted from these beds symbolized the resurrection of life after death.

It was this legend that accounted for Osiris's role as a god of the dead and ruler of the Egyptian underworld. He was associated with funerary rituals, at first only with those of the Egyptian monarch, later with those of the populace in general. The pharaoh was believed to become Osiris after his death. . . . Osiris was also a judge of the dead, referred to as the 'lord of Maat' (i.e., of divine law).

the air shafts remains a mystery but the builders of the pyramid went to great trouble to construct them.

In centuries past, it was believed the shafts had been used by the living to communicate with those who were believed to have been buried alive with the pharaoh inside the pyramid. But since no human remains were found within, this is unlikely.

There are similar air shafts in the Queen's Chamber, although these do not continue to the outside. In 1993, Rudolf Gatenbrink and a team of German archaeologists sent a small robot with a video camera up one of the shafts in the Queen's Chamber. After traveling about 210 feet, the robot was stopped by a stone plug, now known as Gatenbrink's Door, that holds two copper pins whose purpose remains a mystery. What, if anything, lies beyond Gatenbrink's Door remains unknown.

While the air shafts coming from the Queen's Chamber do not continue to the outside, they do appear to have had meaningful alignment with the stars at the time of the pyramid's construction. According to a website about Giza maintained by Felixity Eileen Zollicoffer O'Douglaii:

> [In] approximately 2450 B.C. the shafts . . . were aligned with a constellation and star that both figure prominently in ancient Egyptian texts: the northern shaft was aligned with the constellation Orion (often associated with the Egyptian god Osiris), and the southern shaft was aligned with the star Sirius (associated with the Egyptian goddess Isis).
>
> [In addition] the northern shaft of the Great Pyramid's King's Chamber was aligned to the Pole Star and the southern shaft was aligned to the belt stars of Orion. [39]

With such alignment, modern Egyptologists hypothesize that the shafts had religious purposes, allowing the pharaoh's soul to escape from the pyramid. The northern shaft was meant to take the king to the afterlife in the stars, and the southern shaft was to allow connections to a boat to the sun. These theories, however, remain speculative—the Egyptians believed that the soul could travel through stone walls and would not have needed air shafts to escape to the heavens.

Stairway to Heaven

While some think that the pharaoh's soul might travel up the air shafts, the oblong constellation Orion, with three stars aligned near the middle, has a different meaning for Bauval. In the 1980s, he was taking aerial photographs of the three pyramids at Giza when he noticed something unusual about the alignment of the structures. Bauval consulted colleagues:

> Most of my friends . . . were in the construction industry—civil engineers, architects, planners—and I felt that their opinion might help. My aim was to see if we could agree on the reasons for the odd layout plan of the three pyramids.
>
> As I had thought, most of those who looked at the photograph made the same observation: the three pyramids were each set along their own meridian (north-south) axes and everyone noticed the south-west diagonal along which the two larger pyramids are set. They agreed that this indicated a unified plan. Then came the confusion I had anticipated: they wondered why the third pyramid was so much smaller than the other two, and, even more puzzling, why it was slightly offset east of the south-west diagonal line which linked the two larger pyramids. All agreed that the size and offset of the Menkaure pyramid had been a deliberate choice by the architect. The question was why?[40]

After much thought and consultation, Bauval concluded that Menkaure's pyramid was deliberately smaller and offset from the main axis of the other two, not because the pharaoh lacked the resources to build a larger pyramid as many believed, but because the third star in Orion's "belt" is smaller and slightly

Some people believe that the Giza pyramids were built to correspond to the location of the stars in Orion's "belt" (pictured, center).

set off from the other two. As Bauval explains: "The way the three stars were slanted in relation to the axis of the Milky Way, the offset of the small star from the alignment of the two brighter ones, the southern shaft in Cheops's pyramid targeted to these very stars when the pyramid was built—all this was too much to be coincidence."[41]

Bauval set about proving his theory by consulting the ancient Pyramid Texts. He discovered that the ancient Egyptians considered these stars and the surrounding Milky

63

Way, called a waterway, to be heaven. The pharaohs were supposed to enter heaven at Orion. As the Pyramid Texts state: "[Heaven] has grasped the king's hand at the place where Orion is. . . . O Osiris King . . . Betake yourself to the waterway [Milky Way] . . . may a stairway to [heaven] be set for you at the place where Orion is."[42]

Upon further examination, Bauval concluded that positions of older Fourth Dynasty pyramids such as the Bent Pyramid of Dahshur also corresponded with stars in the Orion constellation.

Since Egyptologists have always suspected that the ancients built a model of heaven on earth, it made sense to Bauval that these pyramid complexes were re-creations of heaven.

Time and Space

Bauval's theory, while not universally accepted, answered the question of why there were no mummified pharaohs or piles of treasure within the pyramids. But it contains a problem that has forced the creation of a new theory about the age of the pyramids that is itself controversial.

The problem is this: The pyramids are believed to have been built around 2550 B.C., but the position of the stars changes over the centuries and the place of Orion in the modern night sky is different from its position during construction forty-six hundred years ago.

Bauval expected the pyramids to correspond with Orion's position during the twenty-sixth century B.C. The researcher was shocked, however, to discover that in reality the pyramids would have aligned with the three stars of Orion many thousands of years earlier, in 10450 B.C. So, while solving one problem—the alignment of the pyramids—Bauval created new problems by calling into question the true age of the structures. In response to this problem Bauval theorized that while the pyramids were probably built around 2550 B.C., they might have been designed many centuries earlier, in 10450 B.C.

Some investigators, however, say that the pyramids truly are older than generally believed. As Reg T. Miller writes in *Pyramid Truth Gateway Universe:*

> Only now, a small group of researchers is beginning to realize that precursor civilizations existed before the Egyptians of five thousand years ago. I submit that there was at least one, and maybe several, existing between 52,000 years ago and 10,000 years ago. Close examination of one remaining artifact of that precursor civilization, the Great Pyramid, reveals building technology that far surpasses what we could accomplish today. The trouble is that the truth is to be found among the often-overlooked subtle details. Most observers are fooled by the cursory observations and conclusions. . . . In truth, the standard theory leaves many enigmas.[43]

This theory is supported by a few researchers, but most dispute it, pointing out that during the last two centuries of archaeological excavations at the pyramids no artifacts, pottery, or inscriptions have been found that are more than five thousand years old.

Built by Aliens?

While Bauval's conclusions provoke more questions than provide answers, there are far more unconventional theories as to the purpose of the pyramids. In fact, some have been so overwhelmed by the complexity of the monuments that they have concluded that neither the ancient Egyptians—nor indeed any humans—could have possibly possessed the tools or technological skills necessary to erect the buildings. These people have deduced that the pyramids were constructed by space aliens.

In 1969 author Erich von Däniken published a runaway best-seller entitled *Chariots of the Gods?* in which he claimed

Erich von Däniken, author of the best-seller Chariots of the Gods?

that only beings with advanced knowledge could have built the Great Pyramid.

He points out, for example, that the building sits exactly at a point of 30° latitude and 30° longitude, which divides the world's continents and oceans into equal halves, placing the pyramid at the exact center of the earth. Von Däniken claims only a race with advanced knowledge of astronomy and navigation could have chosen the spot. The author also claims that the Nile River Valley could never have produced enough food to feed the army of human workers needed to build the pyramid.

Von Däniken suggests that many aspects of Egyptian religious beliefs were inspired by aliens. For example, the idea of the dead pharaohs rising to the stars might have been inspired by people watching spaceships rise into the air. And the idea of an afterlife, so central to ancient Egyptian religion, was inspired by space aliens who instructed the pharaohs to mummify their corpses so that they could be brought back to life at a later time. In other words, not only the pharaoh's spirit but his actual physical body would live forever. Ignoring the fact that few articles of money or jewelry were ever found in the pyramids, von Däniken writes:

> Drawings and sagas actually indicated that the "gods" promised to return from the stars in order to awaken the well-preserved bodies to new life. That is why the provisioning of the embalmed corpses in the burial

chambers took such a practical form and was intended for a life on this side of the grave. Otherwise what were they supposed to have done with money, jewelry, and their favorite articles? . . . [The] point of all the preparations was obviously the continuation of the old life in a new life. The tombs were tremendously

Beyond Human Ability

In the late 1960s, Erich von Däniken proposed that the pyramids were built by space aliens in his best-selling book *Chariots of the Gods?* In the following excerpt, the author attempts to prove that humans could not have built the pyramids.

Is it really a coincidence that the height of the pyramid of Cheops multiplied by a thousand million—98,000,000 miles—corresponds approximately to the distance between the earth and sun? Is it a coincidence that a meridian running through the pyramids divides continents and oceans into two exactly equal halves? Is it coincidence that the area of the base of the pyramid divided by twice its height gives the celebrated figure π [pi]? Is it coincidence that calculations of the weight of the earth were found and is it also coincidence that the rocky ground on which the structure stands is carefully and accurately leveled? . . .

With what power, with what "machines," with what technical resources was the rocky terrain leveled at all? How did the master builders drive the tunnels downward [and] how did they illuminate them? Neither here nor in the rock-cut tombs in the Valley of Kings were torches or anything similar used. There are no blackened ceilings or walls or even the slightest evidence that traces of blackening have been removed. How and with what were the stone blocks cut out of the quarries? With sharp edges and smooth sides? How were they transported and joined together to the thousandth of an inch? Once again there is a wealth of explanations for anyone to choose from. . . .

None of these explanations stands up to a critical examination. The Great Pyramid is and remains visible testimony of a technique that has never been understood. Today, in the twentieth century, no architect could build a copy of the pyramid of Cheops, even if the technical resources of every continent were at his disposal.

durable and solid, almost atom-bomb proof; they could survive the ravages of all the ages. The valuables left in them, gold and precious stones, were virtually indestructible. . . . I am only concerned with the question: Who put the idea of corporeal rebirth into the heads of the [pharaohs]? And whence came the first audacious idea that the cells of the body had to be preserved so that the corpse, preserved in a very secure place, could be awakened to new life after thousands of years?[44]

As to why aliens would bother to preserve the self-aggrandizing kings of ancient Egypt, von Däniken believes that the space travelers might have wanted to preserve men who could remember the specific time in which they lived, living museum pieces who could recite ancient history as if it were part of their everyday lives, which in fact, it was. Otherwise, von Däniken thinks that it would not have occurred to the average ancient to believe in the afterlife, writing:

Where did the idea of immortality come from, and how did people get the concept of corporeal reawakening in the first place? The majority of ancient peoples knew the technique of mummification, and the rich people actually practiced it. I am . . . concerned here . . . with solving the problem of where the idea for a reawakening, a return to life, originated. Did the idea occur to some king or tribal prince purely by chance or did some prosperous citizen watch "gods" treating their corpses with a complicated process and preserving them in bomb-proof sarcophagi? Or did some "gods" (space travelers) transmit to a quick-witted prince of royal blood their knowledge of how corpses can be reawakened after a special treatment?[45]

The Twelfth Planet

Von Däniken attempts to prove that the Egyptians were inspired by space aliens. Researcher Zecharia Sitchin, a

Some researchers theorize that space aliens such as these depicted here constructed the pyramids because the ancient Egyptians could not have possessed the tools or technological skills necessary for such a monumental task.

Russian raised in Palestine, expands on this theory, claiming that the Egyptians were taught to build the pyramids by a superintelligent extraterrestrial race.

Sitchin, a linguist, believes that the Bible is an accurate historical document and the words in the Book of Genesis may be interpreted to mean that space aliens started the human race, telling interviewer Robert Rouse:

> My starting point was . . . the puzzle of who were the Nefilim, that are mentioned in Genesis, Chapter six, as the sons of the gods who married the daughters of Man in the days before the great flood, the Deluge. The word Nefilim is commonly . . . translated "giants".

. . . I questioned [the] interpretation . . . because the word, Nefilim, the name by which those extraordinary beings, "the sons of the gods" were known, means literally, "Those who have come down to earth from the heavens."[46]

Sitchin believes that these "giants" originally lived on the "Twelfth Planet," an as-yet undiscovered planet in the earth's solar system that is numbered as twelve because Sitchin includes the sun and moon in addition to the nine known planets.

According to Sitchin, people from the Twelfth Planet came to earth more than five hundred thousand years ago and the events that followed were recorded in the Book of Genesis. Sitchin says that writings on ancient Sumerian clay tablets identify these people as Anunnaki, whose name means "Those Who from Heaven to Earth Came."[47]

Sitchin recorded his beliefs in a series of books called *The Earth Chronicles.* The second book in the series, *Stairway to Heaven,* claims that the Giza pyramids were actually a spaceport and that the pyramids were landing beacons for the Anunnaki.

Cosmic Debris

Researcher and author Alan Alford also believes in the Anunnaki, but thinks that the Egyptians were inspired by cosmic debris, specifically meteorites. Alford states that the benben stone worshiped at the temple of Heliopolis, located northeast of modern Cairo, was actually a pyramid-shaped meteorite that had fallen to earth. He backs up his theory, like many other researchers have done, by quoting the Pyramid Texts, writing on his website:

The central theme of the Pyramid Texts was that Osiris's body had been dismembered and cast down from heaven to earth. Osiris then came to reside in the underworld—known to the Egyptians as 'the Island of Fire'.

The Egyptians believed that the deceased king could acquire an afterlife in Heaven by becoming one with Osiris. This magical act was effected by the opening-of-the-mouth ceremony. Significantly, the mouth of the mummy was split open by a special tool (an 'adze') which had a blade of meteoric iron.

The purpose of Egyptian religion was to turn back time—to return the meteoric iron to the Sky and reassemble there the iron members of Osiris-the-king, alias Osiris the god.

Having ascended to Heaven, the Egyptian king would spend his afterlife upon a throne of iron.[48]

Alford concludes that the meteorites were originally in an asteroid belt near Neptune that collided with two planets, which then exploded. These destroyed planets had been home to the Anunnaki who then moved to earth and instructed the earthlings to build the pyramids. Again, quoting the Pyramid Texts, Alford states:

These Anunnaki are clearly alluded to in Egyptian texts as the 'Builder Gods', who renovated the foundations of the Earth in millions of places. . . .

It's an awesome thought that our modern culture is not the most advanced on this planet, and that a more advanced race has been here alongside us for thousands of years. But the Great Pyramid and the exploded planet cult of the Egyptians are the evidence that this may indeed be so. And we shouldn't be too dismissive of the idea for there is no reason in principle why a more technologically advanced race cannot live alongside a less technologically advanced race. This is the case today, since we modern folk share a planet with some very primitive tribes, who still live a neolithic life style.[49]

Pyramids on Mars

While some think that extraterrestrials came to earth to build pyramids, others believe they have seen the pyramids—and the Sphinx—on another planet. In 1976 the Viking *Explorer,* launched by the U.S. space agency NASA, took thousands of pictures of the surface of Mars. In the northern desert region called Cydonia a mile-long mesa about fifteen hundred feet high looked to many like huge pyramids and a massive face made from rock. While scientists state unequivocally that the formations are simply created from the natural rock shaped by wind erosion, Richard C. Hoagland, a NASA consultant, disagrees. As Robert C. Kiviat writes in *Omni* magazine:

A 1976 picture taken by the Viking Explorer *shows the so-called "Martian Sphinx" (top right) and "The City" (at left).*

> After analyzing specific [photographic] frames, taken with different sun angles during orbits weeks

apart . . . [Hoagland's] interdisciplinary team of researchers has found substantial evidence that the face, some adjacent pyramid structures, and other objects on Mars' surface were created by intelligent beings.[50]

When the photos were later published on the Internet, a new round of speculation began when some claimed the face resembled the Sphinx, built to guard the pyramids at Giza. And several pyramidlike structures in the area have given rise to a theory that the entire Cydonia area is a stunning replication of the Giza pyramid complex.

If the face was built to resemble the Sphinx, it is very large, about 1.6 miles long, 1.2 miles wide, and a towering 1,300 feet high. Those who believe it is modeled on the guardian of the pyramids (or vice versa), think that it is too symmetrical to have been carved by wind. The Martian Sphinx, as it is called, even seems to be wearing a headpiece similar to the one the Egyptian Sphinx wears.

About twelve miles from the Sphinx-like mountain, an area known as "The City" shows a cluster of pyramid-shaped objects and a "fortress" that shows a pyramid with hollowed sides in a fortlike manner.

Hungry for Answers

The likenesses of the Sphinx and pyramids on Mars have been used by researchers such as Sitchin to "prove" that space aliens were involved with building the pyramids—and even built them on other planets. Like so many researchers before them, authors such as Sitchin, Alford, and von Däniken have molded minute details about the pyramids into amazing theories that leave little room for the assumptions of conventional scholars, who are either dismissed or ignored. Not so coincidentally along the way, these authors have sold hundreds of thousands of books to a public ever-hungry for answers to the riddles of the pyramids.

Whether or not the pyramids were built by sun cults, star cults, extraterrestrials, or simply industrious Egyptians remains to be explained. But from where they sit on a plateau in Giza the pyramids thrusting into the night sky pose a cosmic riddle that leaves more questions than answers.

Chapter 4

Pyramidology and Pyramid Power

The questions of how and why the pyramids were built, and by whom, have inspired fascinating theories ranging from the scientific to the fantastic. While some have credited the construction of the pyramids to ancient Egyptian sun cults and even space aliens, others have spent their lives analyzing, measuring, and meditating on pyramid prophecies and pyramid power. Theories abound that the pyramids can generate electricity, pump water, sharpen razor blades, and even predict the end of the world.

In 1859 an eccentric English publisher named John Taylor—who had never been to Egypt—published a book, *The Great Pyramid: Why Was It Built? And Who Built It?*, that became the foundation of the modern mystical science of "pyramidology"—pyramid prophecy based on readings from the Bible. Taylor was convinced that the architect of the Great Pyramid was not Khufu, but the biblical patriarch Noah.

Taylor studied the geometry of the Great Pyramid at Giza. By dividing the length of the pyramid's sides by two times their height, he came up with 3.144, close to the ratio known as pi. Tompkins explains the mathematical meaning of this discovery: "[The] height of the Pyramid appeared to be in

Researchers have proposed a number of different theories about the significance of the Great Pyramid's dimensions.

relation to the perimeter of its base as the radius of a circle is to its circumference."[51] Since the value of pi was not known in Egypt until 1700 B.C. Taylor concluded that whoever built the pyramids must have had divinely inspired abilities.

Taylor continued his calculations, trying to find some meaning in other dimensions of the pyramid. He found that the number of inches along the base of the pyramid's four sides was 36,600. By dividing the number by 100, he came up with 366, about the number of days in a year. The meaning is explained on the website "A Case of Science, Pseudo-Science and Religion":

> By manipulating the number 366 and other dimensions of the pyramid, he [Taylor] concluded that its builders had used a unit of length which differed from the British inch by only a few thousandths of an inch. Twenty-five of these "pyramid inches" made a "pyramid cubit," and 10 million pyramid cubits approximates the

length of the radius of the earth on its polar axis fairly closely. These and a series of similar calculations provided what Taylor considered to be adequate evidence that the Great Pyramid had been built as a model of the earth, to serve as a record for mankind of the important dimensions and proportions of the globe.[52]

Pyramids and the Bible

In *Secrets of the Great Pyramid*, Peter Tompkins explains the religious beliefs of nineteenth-century founder of "pyramidology" John Taylor:

More than a scholar and a mathematician, Taylor was also a profoundly religious man, thoroughly steeped in the Old Testament which he believed to be literally true. To Taylor the creation of Adam had occurred in 4000 B.C. and the Flood in 2400 B.C. It seemed to him hard to believe that . . . [after the Flood] man could have redeveloped to the point of building so complex a structure as the Great Pyramid. Taylor could come to but one conclusion: whoever had built the Pyramid must have done so under the direct influence of Divine Revelation as Noah had built the Ark. In his own words: "It is probable that to some human beings in the earliest ages of society, a degree of intellectual power was given by the Creator, which raised them far above the level of those succeeding inhabitants of the earth." Taylor even ventured the hypothesis that the builders of the Pyramid were of "the chosen race in the line of, though preceding Abraham; so early indeed as to be closer to Noah than to Abraham." Because of the close similarity of the British inch to the "Pyramid inch," his idea was to give impetus to the theory that the British were related to the Lost Tribes of Israel, "which during their captivity and wanderings preserved a knowledge of the wisdom of the Egyptians." As might have been expected, Taylor, who had been known as a benign and dignified old gentleman, had a hard time convincing his quiet Victorian contemporaries of such wild and revolutionary theories, especially as they were just then being rocked by Darwin's theory of the descent of man.

With these numbers, Taylor hypothesized that whoever built the pyramids wanted to leave a record of mathematics and astronomy that would be easily understood by future generations.

Pyramidology

Near the end of his life, Taylor's theories were taken up by Charles Piazzi Smyth, the Astronomer-Royal of Scotland and a respected member of Britain's prestigious Royal Society. By adapting Taylor's hypotheses to his own calculations, Smyth published several papers and books on pyramidology that did much to popularize the pseudoscience in Europe and the United States.

Unlike Taylor, Smyth journeyed to Egypt to study the Great Pyramid himself, and spent significant time and money to carefully and accurately measure each facet of the structure, the surrounding geography, and the stars overhead. The "Pyramidology" website describes his work:

> Smyth derived a complex set of numerical interrelationships between such things as the number of stones used in the construction of the inner chambers of the pyramid, the volume and shape of the stone coffer found in the King's Chamber of the pyramid, the number of faces and angles of the pyramid, and the number of courses of masonry between various chambers within the pyramid, among many other things. For some reason Smyth considered relationships of involved combinations of numbers such as 25, 50, 10, 366, and 9 as particularly significant. He felt that these numbers were included in the pyramid's dimensions as a record of the "perfect" standards of measurement that God intended man to use.

> Besides linear measurements, Smyth spent much time investigating other physical properties of the pyramid such as the temperature and barometric pressure in the inner chambers and the weight and density of the

stone coffer in the King's Chamber. Again, he derived supposedly important relationships between these measurements, and he concluded that perfect units of weight and temperature were embodied in these dimensions.[53]

Reading great significance into the concept of the pyramid inch, Smyth devised even more confusing calculations, which he imbued with deep significance. For example, he devised a mathematical formula by multiplying the length of the base in pyramid inches (P.inches) to the proportion of the length to the height (10 to 9, or 10^9). With this formula, Smyth came up with 91,840,000, or the approximate distance of the earth from the sun. Although these numbers seem arbitrary, they generated heated debate at the time. In fact, Smyth was the first and only member to ever resign from the Royal Society because they refused to publish his findings.

Pyramidologist Charles Piazzi Smyth believed that the scored lines on the wall of the Descending Passage were intended to be used as a calendar to predict the future.

Calculating the End of the World

Smyth generated more controversy by the meaning he gave to the straight notches, known as "scored lines," that were cut into the wall of the Descending Passage. Smyth believed that these lines were intentionally marked from the floor to the ceiling for use as a calendar that could predict the future.

Using astronomical calculations and biblical passages, Smyth determined that the first line, about forty feet from the entrance of the pyramid, represented the date March 21, 2141 B.C. Concluding that this was the time that the pyramid's "clock"

Debunking Pyramidology

While some people believe Charles Piazzi Smyth's theories about the divine nature of the pyramid, attempts to debunk his assumptions are ongoing. The "Pyramidology, A Case of Science, Pseudo-Science and Religion" website challenges the beliefs of pyramidology:

Many of Smyth's calculations and the [conclusions] he based upon them seem artificial and arbitrary. What, for example, is the significance of the number . . . [he] used in relating the height of the pyramid to the distance of the earth from the sun? What meaning does the number ten million have, other than the fact that there are approximately ten million pyramid inches in the polar radium of the earth? The pyramid is a rich source of the kind of data Smyth worked with, and it would be surprising if he had been unable to come up with some interesting number combinations after manipulating such data.

The general philosophical problem of attaching the proper meaning to [the] evidence is very difficult. . . . John Taylor and Piazzi Smyth were utterly convinced that nearly every detail of the architecture of the Great Pyramid was included intentionally, that is, designed. On the other hand most scientists, historians, and even interested laymen are immediately convinced, upon reading Smyth's claims, that he inferred far too much from the data he gathered.

In addition, Smyth was hardly a dispassionate, objective scientist when dealing with the pyramid. His writings shows that he certainly had a deep emotional commitment to demonstrating "scientifically" that the Christian religion is true, and that he saw his work with the pyramid as a means by which he could do so. . . .

Considering the fact that Smyth made his own measurements, obtaining hundreds of lengths with which to work, and that he spent twenty years mulling over these figures, it is not hard to see how he achieved such remarkable results.

had been set, Smyth measured back and forth from the first scored line and used the numbers in pyramid inches to represent years. Coincidentally, the years Smyth arrived at coincided with stories in the Bible. Examples are provided by Jason Jeffrey on the "Prophecy and the Great Pyramid" website:

Measuring 688 P.inches beyond the Scored Lines, down the Descending Passage, an aperture appears in the roof. This aperture is the entrance to the Ascending Passage, which leads into the Grand Gallery. Progressing 688 years from 2141 B.C. gives the date 1453 B.C., or to be more precise as tests and calculations can prove, the 30th of March, 1453 B.C.

The significance of this date to the early pyramidologists was clear: It marks the date of the Exodus of the Israelites from Egypt, and their receiving the Law, through Moses. A granite plug, at this very point, fills the Ascending Passage. The Granite Plug . . . corresponds to the two blocks of granite that Moses had received the Ten Commandments on the summit of Mount Horeb. . . .

Measuring up the Ascending Passage at the given scale of one P.inch per year, we find that the entrance of the Grand Gallery is marked 1485 P.inches away. . . . 1485 years after 30 March, 1453 B.C. brings us to 1 April, 33 A.D.

This date is said to represent nothing less than the traditionally-recognised [sic] date of the Crucifixion of Jesus the Christ and the sudden 'raising of the roof' at this point refers to human enlightenment, the release of cosmic power, which flowed from that event.[54]

Since the late 1880s, when Smyth published a series of books discussing his findings, these kinds of predictions have been adapted by various authors who claim that the pyramid is a prophecy set in stone. Over the years, claims have been advanced that the dates corresponding to pyramid inches match up with events such as the American Revolution in 1776 and the end of World War II in 1945. In fact, Smyth himself claimed that the scored lines foreshadowed the second coming of Jesus Christ in 1911.

Although most doubt that Jesus returned to earth in 1911, this has not stopped others from expanding on Smyth's theories. In 1981, author Charles Berlitz published his best-selling book *Doomsday 1999 AD*, which predicted the world would end on September 17, 2001, writing, "[It] is still intriguing to observe that certain modern events appear to have been indicated in advance . . . the gallery measurements apparently indicated critical events that corresponded to World War I, World War II, the Atomic Age, and crucial events of the 50s and 70s. But the measurements—and history itself—seem to break off in 2001."[55]

Modeled on Atlantis

While Smyth, Berlitz, and others look to the Bible for explanations of the Great Pyramid, others look to ancient Greece for answers and hold that people from the mythical city of Atlantis built the pyramids.

Around the fourth century B.C., the Greek philosopher Plato wrote of an advanced utopian culture that had once thrived on the island of Atlantis, southwest of continental Europe. A powerful volcanic eruption in 9600 B.C., however, destroyed Atlantis and its people, the Atlantians.

The idea of this advanced society living in perfect harmony flourished over the centuries. Then, in 1882, a Minnesota politician named Ignatius L. Donnelly wrote a book, *Atlantis: The Antediluvian World*, that connected Atlantis to Christianity and the Great Pyramid. In his book Donnelly asks:

> Were not the pyramids of Egypt . . . imitations of similar structures in Atlantis? Might not the building of such a gigantic edifice have given rise to the legends existing on both continents in regard to a Tower of Babel [as mentioned in the Bible]?

> How did the human mind hit upon this singular edifice—the pyramid? By what process of development did it reach it? Why should these extraordinary structures crop out on the banks of the Nile . . . ? And why . . .

should they stand with their sides square to the four cardinal points of the compass? Are they in this, too, a reminiscence of the Cross, and of the four rivers of Atlantis that ran to the north, south, east, and west [as mentioned by Plato]?[56]

Donnelly goes to great lengths to assure readers that Atlantians indeed founded Egyptian civilization and instructed them to build pyramids. To make his point, the author cites Greek mythology, biblical tales, and scientific theories. Donnelly also compares the Egyptian pyramids to those in

Ignatius L. Donnelly wrote that Atlantians, residents of the mythical city of Atlantis, founded Egyptian civilization and built the pyramids.

other regions of the world, such as those built by the Mayans in Central America and the Incas in Peru. As the author states, all of these structures have similar interior passages, are dedicated to the sun, and have similar astronomical orientations. Donnelly believes that only the Atlantians would have had the wherewithal to travel around the world to build these monumental structures.

Pyramid Power

In the early twentieth century, the theories of Donnelly and others were seized by psychics, mediums, and researchers who continued to make claims about the origins of the pyramids and their true meaning. In the early 1930s, however, a new branch of pyramidology began in southern France when Antoine Bovis, a merchant living on the Riviera, began to construct scale-model pyramids with dimensions based on Khufu's tomb.

Bovis had first visited the pyramids around 1920 and, while exploring the King's Chamber, noticed a garbage can containing dead mice, cats, and dogs that had become mummified, but gave off no odor from decay. Bovis asked his guide why the carcasses were stored there and was told that small animals sometimes wander into the pyramid, get lost in the inner chambers, and eventually die of starvation. The local guides pick them up and store them in a receptacle for disposal, as they had been doing for centuries.

Bovis picked up the corpse of a cat, and noticed that the creature's body was extremely light, shrunken, and seemingly mummified. Upon further exploration, he found that the bodies of the other dead animals that had wandered into the pyramid were also mummified.

When he returned home, Bovis constructed a scale-model of the pyramid and aligned it on an exact north-south axis. He placed a small pedestal inside the hollow structure, about one-third of the way up from the base, the same height as the King's Chamber in the Great Pyramid. Bovis placed a dead cat on the pedestal and was astounded to discover that it did not smell, but instead shrank and dried into a mummified corpse.

Over the next several weeks, Bovis discovered that when meat and other items that spoil quickly were placed in the pyramid the moisture was sucked out and the material became dehydrated. He called the mysterious energies of the pyramid radiethesia and theorized that other geometric shapes such as cones, funnels, and squares might also possess such powers.

Bovis wrote about his discoveries and gave lectures to enraptured crowds. When a Czechoslovakian engineer named Karel Drbal read about the Frenchman's experience in a newspaper, he began his own research and discovered that he could mummify meat from cows and sheep, as well as frogs, snakes, and lizards. He even found he could preserve eggs and flowers in his model.

While conducting his experiments, Drbal remembered that during his years in the army, soldiers often repeated the superstitious belief that razor blades left in the moonlight would become dull. Drbal wondered if the pyramid, too, might dull blades in the same way they had reduced the molecules of organic matter. Drbal placed a sharp shaving blade under the pyramid for several days but did not notice any change. When he shaved with it, however, the blade remained miraculously sharp, giving him fifty shaves instead of the normal five. After the blade finally grew dull, he put it back in the pyramid and claimed that it was returned to its sharpened state. Drbal explained this phenomenon by writing:

> There is a relation between the shape of the space inside the pyramid and the physical, chemical and biological processes going on inside that space. By using suitable forms and shapes, we should be able to make processes occur faster or delay them. [57]

The Cheops Pyramid Razor Blade Sharpener

Czechoslovakian engineer Karel Drbal was convinced that dull razor blades became sharper when placed under a model of the Great Pyramid. He was so sure, in fact, that he registered a patent to obtain exclusive rights to his invention, known as the Cheops Pyramid Razor Blade Sharpener. In the application, which is reprinted on the "Republic of Czechoslovakia Office for Patents and Inventions" website, Drbal writes:

> The invention relates to the method of maintaining of razor blades and straight razors sharp without the auxiliary source of energy. To sharpen the blades, therefore no mechanical, thermal, chemical or electrical (From an artificial source) means are being used. . . .

> According to this invention, the blade is placed in earth's magnetic field under a hollow pyramid made of . . . material such as hard paper, paraffin paper, hard cardboard, or some plastic. The pyramid has an opening in its base through which the blade is inserted. This opening can be square, circular, or oval. . . . The razor blade or straight razor is placed on the support made also of . . . material, same as the pyramid, or other such as cork, wood, or ceramics, paraffin, paper, [etc]. Its height is chosen between 1/5 and 1/3 of the height of the pyramid. . . . Although it is not absolutely necessary, it is recommended that the blade be placed on the support with its sharp edges facing west or east respectively, leaving its side edges as well as its longitudinal axis oriented in North South direction. . . .

> When this device was used, 1778 shaves were obtained using 16 razor blades, which is 111 shaves per blade on the average. . . . The lowest count was 51, the highest was 200. It is considered very easy to achieve up to 50 shaves on the average.

Good razor blades were hard to find in Eastern Europe, so in 1959, Drbal tried to patent his Pyramid Razor Sharpener but was first turned down by the patent department. When the head scientist at the department tried it himself, however, Patent No. 91304 was granted to Drbal. Before long, a Czech factory began to sell miniature pyramids made from cardboard. Later they were produced from Styrofoam.

While scientists give no credence to the pyramid razor sharpener, others believe in its mysterious powers. The theory of how such an instrument might work is explained in less-than-scientific terms by Lyall Watson in "Supernature—A Natural History of the Supernatural":

> The edge of a razor has a crystal structure. Crystals are almost alive, in that they grow by reproducing themselves. When a blade becomes blunted, some of the crystals on the edge, where they are only one layer thick, are rubbed off. Theoretically, there is no reason why they should not replace themselves in time. We know that sunlight has a field that points in all directions, but sunlight reflected from an object such as the moon is partly polarised, vibrating mostly in one direction. This could conceivably destroy the edge of a blade left under the moon, but it does not explain the reverse action of the pyramid. We can only guess that the Great Pyramid and its little imitators act as lenses that focus energy or as resonators that collect energy, which encourages crystal growth. The pyramid shape itself is very much like that of a crystal of magnetite, so perhaps it builds up a magnetic field. I do not know the answer, but I do know that it works. My record so far with Wilkinson Sword blades is four months of continuous daily use. [58]

Expanding Pyramid Power

Drbal sold the American rights to his patent to Max Toth, a hypnotist and parapsychologist who studied mental telepathy, clairvoyance, and other unexplained phenomena. In the early 1970s, Toth conducted a series of experiments that he said showed that plant seeds germinated faster when placed under a model pyramid, and the resulting plants were stronger and grew faster.

Toth also recruited human subjects to participate in experiments. These people stated that they felt physically stronger and healthier by simply standing near a model pyramid. Some people with specific ailments placed pyramids near their beds and claimed that they were healed by pyramid power. Toth's subjects also reported feeling a strong energy force in the form of a prickly sensation in their hands when they held them near

A number of experiments were conducted during the 1970s that researchers claimed linked model pyramids with amazing and mysterious powers.

the apex of a model pyramid. In 1974, Toth published his experiments in a book called *Pyramid Power*.

Just as Bovis's experiments had attracted the attention of a respected scientist, Toth's work garnered the attention of G. Pat Flanagan, an electronics genius who holds patents for over two hundred inventions, including a device that allows the deaf to perceive sounds. Flanagan seized on the pyramid concept and wrote his own book called *Pyramid Power*, which contains details of dozens of technical explanations and results of pyramid-based experiments.

Flanagan utilized a process called Kirlian photography that records the radiation emitted by an object, or the "aura" surrounding it in a high-frequency electric field. He found that the leaf of a geranium that was plucked from a plant began to lose its aura and die within thirty minutes. The same leaf, when placed under a pyramid for five minutes, showed an increase in the aura and looked alive and healthy.

Flanagan also discovered in experiments with food that pyramid power changed flavors, writing:

Bitter and sour foods lose their bite, they become milder.

Sweet foods become sweeter.

Coffee loses its bitterness and tastes as if it were acid free. . . .

Acid tasting pineapple loses its acid taste and becomes as sweet as fresh ripe pineapple picked right out of the field. [59]

Flanagan also claimed that the pyramid improves the taste of harsh cigarettes and cheap tobacco.

Other experiments showed that people who sat under pyramids for four hours experienced time distortion and thought that only thirty minutes had passed. The researcher even claimed that his French poodle, which slept under a pyramid every day, soon refused to eat meat and became a canine vegetarian.

Flanagan's book sold more than 1.5 million copies, yet the author could give only vague explanations as to why pyramid power seemed to work, calling it "Biocosmic Energy" which focuses the effects of cosmic radiation on molecular structures.

Power Plants and Water Pumps

By the late 1970s, the New Age spiritual movement was gaining widespread popularity in the United States and Europe, and formerly obscure disciplines such as astrology, psychic healing, and other mystical phenomena became the subjects of dozens of books. Many who participated in this movement had read the works of Toth and Flanagan, and new claims about pyramid power appeared nearly every month. People began constructing tubular pyramids over their beds, their gardens, their doghouses, and even their bathtubs. Utilizing water that had been "charged" under pyramids, people mixed soups, sauces, facial creams, and organic fertilizers.

Although the pyramid fad peaked in the early 1980s, new hypotheses about their powers continued to flourish. Throughout the 1990s, dozens of researchers formulated unique theories about the pyramids.

Expanding on the concept that the pyramids contain "molecular powers," English author Christopher Dunn has proposed that the pyramids not only possess cosmic energy, but manufacture energy, as a giant battery does. A former machinist, Dunn puzzled over the question as to how the pyramids were built only with hand tools. His answer was that the shape and construction of the pyramids utilized the vibrations of the earth and allowed the structures to act as oscillators whose vibrations were converted into electromagnetic energy, or electricity.

Dunn began his work on a trip to Egypt in 1995, where he noticed that some of the artifacts archaeologists had unearthed near the pyramids were so precisely made that they appeared to have been fashioned by sophisticated machines. Dunn had only seen such technical perfection while working with high-tech tools as a skilled machinist in the aerospace industry. He returned to Egypt in 1999 with a high-precision straight edge, square, and radius gauge to measure the corners of a granite box within Khafre's pyramid. Dunn describes the process on his website:

> Climbing into the black granite box that is set into the floor of the chamber, I placed my 12-inch straight edge on the inside surface of the box. . . . I slid this edge along the smooth interior of the granite box with

A man meditates under a tubular pyramid at the World Symposium on Humanity in 1979.

my flashlight shining behind it and demonstrated its exact precision. . . . The squareness of the corners was of critical importance to me. . . .

I wasn't expecting the corners of the sarcophagus to be perfectly square, for perfection is extremely difficult to achieve. However, I was not prepared for the degree of perfection I found. I was flabbergasted as I slid my precision square along . . . and it fit perfectly on the adjacent surface. . . . On three corners the square sat flush against both surfaces. One corner had a gap that was detected by the light test, though it was probably only about .001 inch.[60]

Convinced that only power tools could hew solid granite with such perfection, Dunn contends that the pyramids generated electricity as a modern fuel cell battery does, that is, by converting hydrogen and oxygen into electricity and heat. In Dunn's theory, however, the power is generated in microwaves. This rather complicated theory is explained by Tom Gilmore on "A Brief History of Great Pyramid Egyptology" website:

Dunn proposes that the Queen's Chamber was a reactor producing hydrogen, and the . . . air vents were filled with chemicals [that, when mixed, produced the hydrogen within the chamber]. Dunn suggests a possible chemical mix of hydrated zinc chloride from the north shaft and hydrochloric acid solution in the south shaft. . . .

Dunn claims the dimensions of the pyramid as a fraction of the size of the Earth makes it resonant of the vibration in the [earth's] crust. . . .

[These] vibrations . . . are amplified as a maser [microwave laser], with 27 banks of . . . resonators positioned in the Grand Gallery (accounting for the

27 holes along the gallery floor). The [Descending Passage] with the slots [in the walls] housed baffles for tuning the resonance to one frequency as it passed into the King's Chamber where the coffer . . . acted as a lens focusing . . . cosmic microwaves brought in through the north shaft, amplified by the coffer, and focused to a funnel at the mouth of the south shaft. [61]

While this complex hypothesis is attractive to some, the mystical microwave-powered tools the ancients supposedly used have never been found.

The Water Pump Theory

Dunn is not alone in hypothesizing that the inner chambers of the pyramids were once filled with something other than air. According to a group located in Oregon and known as "The Pharaoh's Pump Foundation," the passages and inner chambers of the Great Pyramid were once used for pumping water. The theory is based on the conclusion that water was the most valuable commodity of the ancient Egyptians, since that country provided a large portion of the food consumed by the ancient world.

According to the foundation's website, the Great Pyramid

is a machine that changed [desert] wasteland into land that groaned with crops or blossomed with roses. The Pyramid Pump meant freedom from want, abundant food, a glorious conquest of environment, and social security. The Great Pyramid was the Ancient's high water mark in mind over matter! Also, water power can be used, and historically has been used to run a wide variety of machinery. [62]

The theory states that water once flowed into the Descending Passage to the Subterranean Chamber. A fire at the top of the Grand Gallery created a vacuum that sucked the water up into the bottom part of the Grand Gallery. The rest of this intricate theory is explained on the organization's website:

> The opening of [a] release valve at the top of the Grand Gallery starts the downward cycle [of the water]. When the release valve is opened, the air and byproducts of the combustion by the fire are replaced by fresh air and the water starts to move back down the Grand Gallery. . . . This moving ponderous column of water lowers and is directed into the Queen's Chamber. . . . The compressed air stores energy that is used to push water up into the King's Chamber. This action compresses air in the upper part of the King's Chamber and water is pushed out of the pump through the [air shafts]. . . . The discharge tubes in the King's Chamber are located in the wall about 5 feet high. Above that, air is compressed by the water coming from the Queen's Chamber. This compressed air in this secondary chamber forces the water out of the discharge tubes. [63]

While it is unclear how this water was directed away from the pyramid, the Pharaoh's Pump Foundation believes that the water power might have been used to irrigate, drive tools such as lathes, and create hydraulic power to move huge blocks of stone used to build the other nearby pyramids.

"Something About the Pyramids"

Ideas about water pumps, giant fuel cells, and biblical prophecy are among the thousands of dreams and theories surrounding the pyramids. While most scholars dismiss these wild theories out of hand, the debate proves that even in the modern world, monuments such as the pyramids—instantly recognizable as the apex of ancient civilization's awesome accomplishments—retain their fascination and refuse to yield answers to the mysteries of design and purpose.

Whether or not extraterrestrials built the Egyptian pyramids, the cost and technological resources needed to reconstruct the monuments today would require an effort akin to sending an astronaut to Mars. Though some have tried to build scale models of the pyramids, none have succeeded. So while the mysteries of the pyramids remain, theories about the pyramids abound. In fact so many have put forth far-out theories that the Egyptologists call these people "pyramidiots."

The Egyptian pyramids are technological marvels that continue to baffle researchers.

Whatever the case, the fact that people are still discussing the pyramids nearly forty-six hundred years after they were built, proves that these amazing structures continue to provide the ancient pharaohs with the eternal life they so desired.

Notes

Introduction: Mysteries in Stone

1. Robert Bauval and Adrian Gilbert, *The Orion Mystery: Unlocking the Secrets of the Pyramids.* New York: Crown, 1994, pp. 2–3.

Chapter One: How Were the Pyramids Built?

2. Mark Lehner, *The Complete Pyramids.* London: Thames and Hudson, 1997, p. 13.
3. David Roberts, "Age of Pyramids," *National Geographic,* January 1995, p. 11.
4. Quoted in Bauval and Gilbert, *The Orion Mystery,* p. 21.
5. Roberts, "Age of Pyramids," p. 14.
6. Lehner, *The Complete Pyramids,* p. 100.
7. "Bent Pyramid," www.crystalinks.com/bentpyr.html.
8. Herodotus, *History.* Chicago: University of Chicago Press, 1987, p. 185.
9. Bauval and Gilbert, *The Orion Mystery,* p. 2.
10. "Mysteries: The Great Pyramid," Modern Mysteries website, http://m155.ryd.student.liu.se/article.php?sid=18, 2000.
11. "Mysteries: The Great Pyramid," Modern Mysteries website.
12. "Mysteries: The Great Pyramid," Modern Mysteries website.
13. Lehner, *The Complete Pyramids,* p. 108.
14. Lehner, *The Complete Pyramids,* p. 108.
15. Roberts, "Age of Pyramids," p. 15.
16. Bauval and Gilbert, *The Orion Mystery,* p. 48.
17. Bauval and Gilbert, *The Orion Mystery,* p. 50.
18. "Are Pyramids Made Out of Concrete?" www.geopolymer.org/archaeo1a.html.
19. Mark Lehner, "This Old Pyramid," NOVA Online Transcripts, www.pbs.org/wgbh/nova/transcripts/1915mpyramid.html, June 2001.

Chapter Two: The Inner Chambers

20. Lehner, *The Complete Pyramids,* p. 92.
21. Lehner, *The Complete Pyramids,* p. 87.
22. Lehner, *The Complete Pyramids,* p. 92.
23. Roberts, "Age of Pyramids," p. 28.
24. Bauval and Gilbert, *The Orion Mystery,* pp. 42–43.
25. Bauval and Gilbert, *The Orion Mystery,* p. 44.
26. Lehner, *The Complete Pyramids,* p. 137.
27. I. E. S. Edwards, *The Pyramids of Egypt.* London: Penguin Books, 1993, pp. 161, 163.
28. Charles Freeman, *The Legacy of Ancient Egypt.* New York: Facts On File, 1997, p. 98.
29. Edwards, *The Pyramids of Egypt,* p. 176.
30. Michael Birrell, "Pyramid Texts," www.museum.mq.edu.au/eegypt2/ptexts.html.
31. Quoted in Bauval and Gilbert, *The Orion Mystery,* p. 64.

32. Bauval and Gilbert, *The Orion Mystery,* p. 66.

Chapter Three: The Pyramids and the Stars

33. Bauval and Gilbert, *The Orion Mystery,* p. 26.
34. Roberts, "Age of Pyramids," pp. 14–15.
35. Peter Tompkins, *Secrets of the Great Pyramid.* New York: Harper & Row, 1971, p. 122.
36. Tompkins, *Secrets of the Great Pyramid,* p. 147.
37. Tompkins, *Secrets of the Great Pyramid,* p. 151.
38. Tompkins, *Secrets of the Great Pyramid,* p. 152.
39. Felixity Eileen Zollicoffer O'Douglaii, "Giza," www.toad.net/~lefay/egypt/giza.html#bauval.
40. Bauval and Gilbert, *The Orion Mystery,* pp. 107–108.
41. Bauval and Gilbert, *The Orion Mystery,* p. 117.
42. Quoted in Bauval and Gilbert, *The Orion Mystery,* p. 116.
43. Reg T. Miller, *Pyramid Truth Gateway Universe.* Blue Hill, ME: Medicine Bear Publishing, 1997, p. 87.
44. Erich von Däniken, *Chariots of the Gods?* New York: G.P. Putnam's Sons, 1969, p. 102.
45. Von Däniken, *Chariots of the Gods?* p. 104.
46. Robert K. Rouse, "Interview with Zecharia Sitchin," www.metatron.se/asitch.html, July 29, 1993.
47. Rouse, "Interview with Zecharia Sitchin."
48. Alan F. Alford, "Exploded Planets," Mysteries of the World, www.eridu.co.uk/Author/Exploded_Planets/exploded_planets.html, 2000.
49. Alan F. Alford, "The Mystery of the UFOs," Mysteries of the World, www.eridu.co.uk/Author/Mysteries_of_the_World/UFOs/ufos.html, 2000.
50. Robert C. Kiviat, "Casting a New Light on the Mars Face," *Omni,* August 1994, p. 31.

Chapter Four: Pyramidology and Pyramid Power

51. Tompkins, *Secrets of the Great Pyramid,* p. 70.
52. "Pyramidology," A Case of Science, Pseudo-Science and Religion, www.greatdreams.com/pyramid.htm.
53. "Pyramidology," A Case of Science, Pseudo-Science and Religion.
54. Jason Jeffrey, "Prophecy and the Great Pyramid," *New Dawn Magazine,* www.newdawnmagazine.com/Articles/Prophecy%20and%20the%20Great%20Pyramid.html, 2001.
55. Quoted in Jeffrey, "Prophecy and the Great Pyramid," *New Dawn Magazine.*
56. Ignatius L. Donnelly, Part IV, Chapter V, The Pyramid, the Cross, and the Garden of Eden, www.sacred-texts.com/atl/ataw/ataw405.htm, 1882.
57. Quoted in Lyall Watson, "Supernature—A Natural History of the Supernatural," www.st-and.ac.uk/~jewsoc/pyramid.html.
58. Watson, "Supernature—A Natural History of the Supernatural."

59. G. Pat Flanagan, *Pyramid Power*. Marina del Rey, CA: De Vorss, 1974, p. 87.
60. Christopher Dunn, "Return to the Giza Power Plant," www.gizapower.com/articles/return.html, 1999.
61. Tom Gilmore, "A Brief History of Great Pyramid Egyptology," www.tomgilmore.com/egyptol.htm, 2001.
62. "The Pharaoh's Pump Foundation," www.thepump.org/faq.html, 1999–2000.
63. "The Pharaoh's Pump Foundation."

For Further Reading

W. R. Akins, *The Secret Power of the Pyramids.* New York: Franklin Watts, 1980. Written at the peak of the pyramid fad, this book covers the building of the pyramids, the rise of "pyramid power" in modern times, and instructions for building scale-model pyramids.

R. O. Faulkner, trans., *The Ancient Egyptian Book of the Dead.* New York: Macmillan, 1985. A mesmerizing book that transcends centuries with 181 spells from the *Book of the Dead,* translated into English and illustrated with photos of papyrus scrolls from which the spells were taken.

Charles Freeman, *The Legacy of Ancient Egypt.* New York: Facts On File, 1997. A fascinating book on the wonders of ancient Egypt with hundreds of beautiful color photographs and interesting facts about everyday life, the wonders of the pharaohs, myths of the gods and goddesses, and archaeological expeditions in the modern era.

Tim McNeese, *The Pyramids of Giza.* San Diego: Lucent Books, 1997. A well-written explanation of Egyptian religion and the widely accepted theories of how the pyramids were built.

Michael O'Neal, ed., *Pyramids.* San Diego: Greenhaven Press, 1995. A title in the Opposing Viewpoints series, this book presents various opinions as to who built the pyramids, and how and why they were built.

James Putnam, *Pyramid.* New York: Knopf, 1994. An Eyewitness Book about the pyramids with easy-to-read text and dozens of full-color photographs.

David Roberts, "Age of Pyramids," *National Geographic,* January 1995. An article about daily life in the age of the pyramid builders and how the ancient kingdom was united by the nearly impossible task of building the monuments.

Brenda Smith, *Egypt of the Pharaohs.* San Diego: Lucent Books, 1996. A detailed and informative book for young adults about life in ancient Egypt.

The Editors of Time-Life Books, *Egypt: Land of the Pharaohs.* Alexandria, VA: Time-Life Books, 1992. Informative text accompanied by hundreds of high-quality photographs and drawings of ancient Egyptian tombs, monuments, pyramids, and artifacts, from the Time-Life Lost Civilizations series.

Works Consulted

Robert Bauval and Adrian Gilbert, *The Orion Mystery: Unlocking the Secrets of the Pyramids*. New York: Crown, 1994. The authors spent more than a decade studying the pyramids and the ancient writings contained within and formed a theory that the ancient Egyptians believed that the pyramids were a reconstruction of heaven on earth and served as a gateway for the pharaohs' souls to travel to the stars.

I. E. S. Edwards, *The Pyramids of Egypt*. London: Penguin Books, 1993. An in-depth study of the pyramids by one of the world's most respected Egyptologists.

G. Pat Flanagan, *Pyramid Power*. Marina del Rey, CA: De Vorss, 1974. A book with details of dozens of technical explanations and results of pyramid power experiments.

Herodotus, *History*. Chicago: University of Chicago Press, 1987. First published in the fifth century B.C., this invaluable work by the Greek historian Herodotus explores ancient Egyptian culture from the perspective of ancient Greece.

Robert C. Kiviat, "Casting a New Light on the Mars Face," *Omni*, August 1994. An article about the mysterious shapes on the planet Mars that resemble the pyramids and the Sphinx.

Mark Lehner, *The Complete Pyramids*. London: Thames and Hudson, 1997. A comprehensive exploration of the pyramids with pictures, maps, drawings, and all manner of interesting information about the massive Egyptian monuments. Written by a renowned professor of Egyptian archaeology.

Reg T. Miller, *Pyramid Truth Gateway Universe*. Blue Hill, ME: Medicine Bear Publishing, 1997. A New Age collection of theories surrounding the pyramids including UFO abductions, time travel, pyramid power, ancient astronauts, and other far-out ideas.

Peter Tompkins, *Secrets of the Great Pyramid*. New York: Harper & Row, 1971. The history of archaeological explorations of the Great Pyramid, including various theories about the mathematical and astronomical designs of the monument that have emerged over many centuries.

Max Toth, and Greg Nielsen, *Pyramid Power: The Secret Energy of the Ancients Revealed*. New York: Destiny Books, 1985. Originally published in 1974, this is the first of many books exploring the perceived abilities of pyramid-shaped objects to preserve food, heal the body, and sharpen dull blades.

Erich von Däniken, *Chariots of the Gods?* New York: G.P. Putnam's Sons, 1969. A 1970s best-seller that claims that aliens were involved in the construction of the pyramids in Egypt as well as the pyramid-like structures in Central and South America.

Internet Sources

Alan F. Alford, "Exploded Planets," Mysteries of the World, www.eridu.co.uk/Author/Exploded_Planets/exploded_planets.html, 2000. Theories about meteorites and pyramids by a researcher and author who has written three books on ancient mythology and wisdom, archaeological anomalies, and the connection of world religions to UFOs.

Alan F. Alford, "The Mystery of the UFOs," Mysteries of the World, www.eridu.co.uk/Author/Mysteries_of_the_World/UFOs/ufos.html, 2000. An interview in which the author talks about extraterrestrials, mythical exploded planets, and the pyramids.

"Are Pyramids Made Out of Concrete?" www.geopolymer.org/archaeo1a.html. A site maintained by the French-based Geopolymer Institute presents theories that challenge commonly held assumptions about the pyramids.

"Bent Pyramid," www.crystalinks.com/bentpyr.html. A site dedicated to the mystery surrounding the first true pyramid.

Michael Birrell, "Pyramid Texts," www.museum.mq.edu.au/eegypt2/ptexts.html. A page about the hieroglyphs discovered in the late Fifth Dynasty as part of a comprehensive website run by the Museum of Ancient Cultures at Macquarie University in Sydney, Australia, with links to articles about funerary customs, dynasties, pyramid construction, and dozens of other subjects related to ancient Egypt.

Ignatius L. Donnelly, Part IV, Chapter V, The Pyramid, the Cross, and the Garden of Eden, www.sacred-texts.com/atl/ataw/ataw405.htm, 1882. The entire text of the nineteenth-century book *Atlantis: The Antediluvian World*, linking the lost city of Atlantis to the pyramids and the Christian religion.

Karel Drbal, "Republic of Czechoslovakia Office for Patents and Inventions," www.amasci.com/freenrg/tors/drbl.html, 1959. A site from the Czechoslovakia Office for Patents and Inventions with the verbatim application for Drbal's Pyramid Razor Blade Sharpener.

Christopher Dunn, "Return to the Giza Power Plant," www.gizapower.com/articles/return.html, 1999. A website advancing the author's hypothesis that, while being built, the pyramids converted the vibrations of the earth into electricity that powered tools to aid in their own construction.

Tom Gilmore, "A Brief History of Great Pyramid Egyptology,"www.tomgilmore.com/egyptol.htm, 2001. Brief biographies and pyramid theories by writers from Herodotus to Charles Piazzi Smyth to Christopher Dunn.

Aymen Ibrahem, "Part II: The Hermopolitan Cosmogony," Egyptian Cosmology, www.eclipse-chasers.com/egypt5.htm, 2000. Theories of a professional astronomer from Egypt concerning solar eclipses and the pyramids.

Jason Jeffrey, "Prophecy and the Great Pyramid," *New Dawn Magazine*, www.newdawnmagazine.com/Articles/Prophecy%20and%20the%20Great%20Pyramid.html, 2001. An article about Charles Piazzi Smyth's pyramidology calculations on a website that, according to its mission statement, is "a journal of alternative news & information."

Mark Lehner and Zahi Hawass, "Who Built the Pyramids?" www.pbs.org/wgbh/nova/pyramid/explore/builders.html, 1997. An interview with Egyptologist Mark Lehner, who explains the failure of a team of modern workers to reconstruct a scale-model pyramid using primitive tools.

"Mysteries: The Great Pyramid," Modern Mysteries website, http://m155.ryd.student.liu.se/article.php?sid=18, 2000. A site about Khufu's pyramid as part of a series about mysterious phenomena.

Felixity Eileen Zollicoffer O'Douglaii, "Giza," www.toad.net/~lefay/egypt/giza.html#bauval. A page that describes the author's tour of the Great Pyramid of Khufu and the Sphinx.

"Osiris, God of the Underworld and Vegetation," http://sobek.colorado.edu/LAB/GODS/index.html. A site run by the Social Science Data Lab at the University of Colorado at Boulder with links to twenty-five "biographies" of Egyptian deities, each profiling a god or goddess and his or her meaning and place in ancient mythology.

"The Pharaoh's Pump Foundation," www.thepump.org/pump.html, 1999–2000. A website dedicated to the theory that the Great Pyramid was once a highly efficient water pump that irrigated the desert.

"The Pharaoh's Pump Foundation," www.thepump.org/faq.html, 1999–2000. The FAQ page of the above website.

"Priest Caste," Ancient Egyptian Culture website, http://emuseum.mankato.msus.edu/prehistory/egypt/religion/priest.html. The EMuseum site, maintained by Minnesota State University, contains links to daily life in ancient Egypt including art, military matters, architecture, hieroglyphs, religion, maps, history, archaeology, and book references.

"Pyramidology," A Case of Science, Pseudo-Science and Religion, www.greatdreams.com/pyramid.htm. A site that attempts to debunk the religious theories surrounding pyramidology.

"Pyramids—The Inside Story," NOVA Online, www.pbs.org/wgbh/nova/pyramid, 1997. The home page of the NOVA television series of the Public Broadcasting System (PBS), with intriguing links that allow readers to explore the pyramids, observe the excavations, look at maps, find updates, and see cross-sections of the Sphinx and the pyramids of Khufu and Khafre. Includes links to Egypt's Pyramid Age, history of Giza, who built the pyramids, and other sites.

Robert K. Rouse, "Interview with Zecharia Sitchin," www.metatron.se/asitch.html, July 29, 1993. An interview with a researcher who claims that space aliens imparted the wisdom of the pyramids to the Egyptians.

"This Old Pyramid," NOVA Online Transcripts, www.pbs.org/wgbh/nova/transcripts/1915mpyramid.html, June 2001. The transcript from the Public Broadcasting System series, in which Professor Joseph Davidovits mixes a concrete aggregate from Egyptian limestone while attempting to prove that the pyramids were constructed from molded concrete.

Lyall Watson, "Supernature—A Natural History of the Supernatural," www.st-and.ac.uk/~jewsoc/pyramid.html. A site with excerpts from the author's book exploring pyramid power.

Index

Picture Credits

Cover photo: ©Roger Ressmeyer/CORBIS
©AFP/CORBIS, 19
AP Photo/Enric Marti, 44
©Mario Beauregard/CORBIS, 88
©Bettmann/CORBIS, 27, 31
©CORBIS, 63
Digital Stock, 15, 95
Fortean Picture Library, 57, 66
Dr. Elmar R. Grubar/Fortean Picture Library, 43
©Erich Lessing/Art Resource, NY, 59
Library of Congress, 39
NASA Photo, 72
Nimatallah/Art Resource, NY, 24, 55
©Richard T. Nowitz/CORBIS, 76
PhotoDisc, 9
©Roger Ressmeyer/CORBIS, 91
Réunion des Musées Nationaux/Art Resource, NY, 17
Stock Montage, Inc., 13, 79, 83
Werner Forman Archive/Art Resource, NY, 21, 48
©Darren Winter/CORBIS, 69

About the Author

Stuart A. Kallen is the author of more than 150 nonfiction books for children and young adults. He has written on topics ranging from the theory of relativity to rock-and-roll history to life on the American frontier. In addition, Mr. Kallen has written award-winning children's videos and television scripts. In his spare time, Stuart A. Kallen is a singer/songwriter/guitarist in San Diego, California.